SOLVE ALL YOUR PROBLEMS
OF WORK, LOVE OR POTENTIAL SUCCESS!

DISCOVER THE FASCINATING ART
OF PREDICTING THE FUTURE!

LEARN TO USE THE ANCIENT KNOWLEDGE
OF THE AMAZING *I CHING!*

This book provides full instruction for the use of the fabled Oriental classic, explaining all 64 of the hexagrams, the symbolic figures upon which the predictions are based. It also tells what the I CHING is and how it was developed, revealing . . .

- *The Unique Uses Of The "I Ching" Through History*
- *The Mystic Principle Behind The Coin Oracle*
- *The Ancient Truth Of The Images*
- *The Proven Power Of Foretelling The Future*
- *The Unusual System Of Personalized Advice And Counsel*

Let the I CHING put you in touch with the rhythms of change, helping you to swim with the tides, not against them.

THE NATURE
OF THE
I CHING

Its Usage and Interpretation

Charles Poncé

AWARD BOOKS
NEW YORK · TANDEM BOOKS
LONDON

FIRST AWARD PRINTING 1970

To Jabir

*That a door may be open
for now and all eternity*

AWARD BOOKS are published by
Universal Publishing and Distributing Corporation
235 East Forty-fifth Street, New York, N. Y. 10017

TANDEM BOOKS are published by
Universal-Tandem Publishing Company Limited
14 Gloucester Road, London SW7, England

Manufactured in the United States of America

ABOUT THE AUTHOR:

Charles Poncé majored in comparative religion at Columbia University and has been studying the I CHING for 15 years. For the past two years he has been giving seminars on the I CHING and its usage, lecturing in colleges throughout the East and giving classes of instruction and interpretation. He has published many articles on the I CHING and has also written on the philosophical tradition behind alchemy in "Ikon," a New York magazine.

CONTENTS

PREFACE

This is the type of book that demands the reader first browse through it, familiarizing himself with what lies ahead. Only then should he settle down to reading—one chapter at a time.

Of the several translations of the *I Ching,* or *Book of Changes,* available, I recommend the Richard Wilhelm translation, rendered into English by Cary F. Baynes and published by the Princeton University Press (the Bollingen edition). I also suggest that the Legge translation be used in conjunction with the above for its sometimes illuminating footnotes and presentation of certain aspects of ancient Chinese culture pertinent to *I Ching* interpretation.

For those with a reading knowledge of Chinese, the two-volume set by Z. D. Sung (China Modern Education Company, Shanghai, 1934–35) contains the original text.

In this handbook the reader will find references to the idea that the *Book of Changes* contains within it a system of spiritual or psychological transformation. Of course, in a book of this scope and size a detailed presentation of the system is not possible. However, a careful application of the few principles mentioned here should reveal the entire system to the individual. Another point to be considered is that the material presented in this book need not be applied every time one attempts to read a hexagram. All methods of interpretation should be thought of as layers to be lifted and employed only when the *I Ching* does not speak to the reader directly. Then, the lifting of a layer, or several layers, will bring him closer to an answer.

The reader should realize that whatever is discussed in this little book must in the last analysis be subject to the intuitions and insights he may attain during *his* dialogue with the *I Ching*. Symbols cannot be revised, they can only be amplified. Therefore, it is necessary that all who take up this interpretation of so mysterious and complex a work keep in mind that it is the product of one man's experience, and that the worth of his experience can only be measured by the extent to which it causes others to seek and create further interpretation.

Throughout, I am heavily indebted to the works of Mircea Eliade, Lama Ananda Govinda, Heinrich Zimmer, Richard and Helmut Wilhelm, and Dr. C. G. Jung.

INTRODUCTION

"Every separate man possesses the one Supreme Ultimate."

The *I Ching* is essentially an instrument of transformation. Its aim is to aid the individual in his attempts at reconciling the dissident elements of his being, to show him the way into the Way where he might discover the process of interior spiritualization. Its presentation of this process is unique in that while revealing to the individual the correctness or incorrectness of his life during any moment in his history, it quietly leads him toward the hidden unity within, managing to achieve this without demanding he adhere to any fixed societal formula. It leaves such matters to the conscience and creativity of the individual. To understand the *I Ching*, how it works and why, we must first understand the concept of the archetypes.

The concept is by no means new. Many philosophers of both past and present have based their systems on such a concept. Of the ancient systems, the most familiar to us is Plato's doctrine of forms or ideas. Ideas were understood as being objective essences existing in a world of their own, original models of all that exists in the world. In other words, each type of class or being was thought of as patterned after an idea. According to this theory there is an ideal idea or form of a man, a tree, a building, etc. The source of these ideas or forms was regarded as the one, the supreme idea in which all multiplicity is contained in harmony.

At about the same time Plato was formulating this theory, the Chinese were also shaping a concept of the archetype and its realm. The one or supreme idea became in their system the Tao or supreme ultimate out of which all things had been born and in which all things were contained in unity. As we shall see in Chapter 5, On the Trigrams (the eight three-lined figures of the *I Ching*), the ideas or forms of Plato find their equivalent in the trigrams for, as the *I Ching* tells us, the trigrams are the models after which all things are patterned.

The twentieth-century view now held by many but first researched and realized by Dr. C. G. Jung, is that the archetypes are psychic structures, dynamic principles of the mind. Plato's theory of the archetypes had them as existing outside and beyond the immediate plane of man's reality. Although affecting man, they were really qualities of the universe having nothing to do with his psychic or physical constitution. They were operative forces expressing universal principles which, in a way, were little more than heavenly mandates. The Chinese, on the other hand, eventually came to understand the trigrams and the original unity, the Tao, to reside within man as components of the mind.

An example from the tenth-century Chinese philosopher Chang Tsai is an apt case in point:

The universe is filled with molds and forms. One cannot examine the universe's systems and principles without intellectual clarity. Given a physical form, one may work back towards that which is hidden, and when a physical form is not present, one may then work back towards the cause of the thing manifested.

For the time being we should take note only of the *first* sentence of this quote; the remainder will be referred to again when we discuss the idea of original mind, below.

This somewhat corresponds to the twentieth-century understanding of the archetypes as constituents of a transpersonal realm of unity now referred to as the objective psyche and understood as operating within the individual. Whether the realm does indeed exist as Plato and others saw it, outside of us, is a philosophical and religious problem of no mean proportion. Regardless of whether it does or not, the important point is that man comes to be influenced by the archetypal realm within the context of an inner and subjective experiencing of himself as well as of the world. Another important distinction made by twentieth-century researchers is the fact that the individual's relationship with the world, with others, and with himself, determines whether these forces will be experienced as benevolent or malevolent forces. The forces themselves are not concerned with specifically expressing themselves as malevolent or benevolent.

In all three theories—Plato's, the Oriental's, and twentieth-century science's—there is one point of agreement: Man is affected by the emanations or forces produced by something akin to an original unity, if not the original unity itself.

As now defined, the archetypes are psychic structures shaped and activated by the libido or psychic energy. Such terms as libido, psychic energy, or any other term used in contemporary psychology and philosophy that refers us to the idea of a quantum of energy residing within the individual corresponds to what was at one time called spirit. The manner in which this energy activates and fills out the archetypes is a simple one and one which has many analogies in nature, especially in the vegetable kingdom.

In winter, the energy that caused a plant to flower and reproduce itself retreats into the ground, toward the root system, leaving behind a brittle and to all appearances dead stalk. The plant's stalk in winter might be likened to the archetype. The specific form of the plant, the configuration of branches and twigs (its form in the Platonic sense) has permanence. It is not until certain conditions in nature occur that the energy residing underground flows back up into the stalk and stems and the plant becomes active again.

In the psyche much the same thing occurs. The archetypes lie between the pool of undifferentiated energy commonly known as the libido, the impersonal sphere of the individual's psyche, and all those components we associate with consciousness—the ego, sense, etc., or the personal sphere. When the individual is confronted with a specific life situation, psychic energy flows into the corresponding archetype, activating it and thereby determining the type of action the individual will or should take.

I

The classic example of an activated archetype and the power it has in shaping the individual's life is found in Freud's concept of the Oedipal complex. According to that theory, every male child passing through the phallic stage—that period when the focal point for libidinal energy is the genital zone—is fated, in fantasy, to kill his father and gain possession of his mother. According to Freud, the repression of these natural impulses in time leads to psychic difficulties. Accepting this psychological premise we may interpret the theory to mean that ways of acting or relating to the world are genetically transmitted and are inherent propensities of the human mind.

The nascent order of the primitive psyche found correspondence in the rhythms of natural phenomena. The "form" each psychic component assumed was selected from the sensory experience of man. As with the dried plant stalk in winter, it is only the form of the archetype that is genetically transmitted. It is the *form* of the father archetype that is inherited, not the image itself. The form takes on visible proportions only when an instant in the world corresponds with an aspect of the archetype. One may here ask how such a thing can occur, how a *pattern* of action and nothing more can be transmitted. Again we are presented with the Westerner's need to make the invisible tangible before accepting it. As impossible and outlandish as the theory of the transmission of form, of ways of action, sounds, science has recently discovered it to be a reality.

In recent experiments, flatworms that had been taught to run a maze were chopped up and fed to a control group that had not as yet been so instructed. This control group when later run through the same maze bettered the original learning-time score of their predecessors. Information had thus been transmitted: The impress of experience had become a part of the organism of the flatworm—enough so that the structure, the *form* of the information, was passed along by the very meat of the organism.

Because the flatworm is the lowest organism on the phylogenetic scale capable of displaying an ability to learn, and because it possesses a human, synaptic-type nervous system, there is every reason to believe that the manner by which information is recorded and retained in this crude organism parallels the human experience.

Professor James V. McConnell of the University of Michigan, in presenting a possible cause of such memory transference, writes:

Hyden, the Swedish biologist, was one of the first to theorise that ribonucleic acid (RNA) might be the complex molecule which served as the chemical mediator of learning. Hyden reasons that if DNA, which is considered exceptionally stable and unchangeable, encoded an organism's "racial" memories, perhaps RNA, which is known to be much more malleable, could act to encode an organism's individual memories; hence RNA would be what is now called the "memory molecule." [Reprint from *New Scientist*, Vol. 21, pp. 456–68]

In the light of these experiments it is obvious that we must seek to redefine the concept of memory. At present, memory is understood to be the residue of an experiential event in the life of an individual, the restricted and personal recordings of a personality, the information of remembered moments. When I die the events experienced on a particular day in a particular year I found to be noteworthy or significant enough to be retained die with me.

The information transmitted from worm to worm in the above mentioned experiments had little to do with the transmission of personality factors. It must now be understood that a physiological condition exists wherein the impress of information on the psyche has nothing to do with the ego. This distinction will have to be emphasized, for here we find the cause of the difficulty people have in accepting the theory of the archetypes. As long as this distinction is not made and understood, the archetypes will be thought of as actually transmitting elements of personality. However, what is recorded is *form,* or pure "way of acting." When the personality dies, personal memory dies—but the outline, the form of recorded information may not.

The flatworm is an extremely simple creature, but in its simplicity, in its similarity with the basic cellular structure of man, it has taught us an important lesson: At one time, apparently, in the early history of mankind, knowledge acquired through an experience in the world became a structural form within the organism to be transmitted along with the other pieces of information the DNA structure contains, i.e., blood type, hair, eye, and skin coloration, specific facial features, bone structure, etc. The archetypal form we have been discussing has, in essence, been proven to be a reality.

Another quality of the archetypes is that they have a tendency first to be discovered *in* the world; that is, psychic energy tends to become personified and thought of as residing outside the individual before it is realized as a component of personality. The pantheons of gods and spirits man once believed existed *in* the world are now recognized as having been the archetypes projected.

In the history of the development of consciousness, the identification of the individual's psyche and its operations with the world is considered the first stage in the evolutionary process. In the second developmental stage, a distinction between what is "real," measurable, and therefore factual, and the "unreal," immeasurable, and, therefore, undemonstrable, occurs. This event took place in the western world between the seventeenth and eighteenth centuries of our era and signaled the birth of science.

To understand this event and its implications, I here present the three phases of the second developmental stage in the evolution of consciousness.

The first phase is that in which the subject-object relationship is discovered. During this period there occurs the painful process of reevaluating, of being torn away from values one had found justification for in phenomena.

The second phase has to do with a despiritualization of the world. Here, natural phenomena are recognized for what they are. Magic, spiritualism, and religion lose their place to science. A distinction between what is real and what is unreal is finally made. The entire time of this stage is spent in testing, measuring, and explaining. Nature is controlled by man. Man is no longer controlled and dictated to by nature, as in the first stage of consciousness. Despiritualization is total, to the point where anyone who admits to believing forces exist beyond the realm of immediate experience is thought of as foolish, if not insane.

One of the fascinating things about the second phase is that man suddenly realizes that he himself is phenomena, that he is a biological organism subject to certain laws. The theory of the unconscious comes into being. Suddenly, the pantheon of gods and demons and spirits that were kicked out of the world is found in man. The evil spirits of yesteryear are given new names: neurosis, psychosis, schizophrenia, catatonia, etc.

The third phase returns us to the conflict experienced in the first phase, but in reverse: In this phase the realization is made that even though we found that the forces operative in the world and universe were not gods and spirits existing "out there," the cause of this mistaken belief has not disappeared. If anything, it has returned to homebase—to the psyche that originally projected them. This realization actually begins somewhere in the second phase, for it is there that a further demarcation is made, there that another dimension of experience becomes a reality—to become the science of psychology.

In the third phase science and metaphysics again become united, but with a significant distinction: It is realized that the newly won knowledge of reality can in no way be threatened, immersed in, and clouded over by an acceptance of the existence of a transpersonal realm of being. If anything, it is enhanced and given meaning beyond that achieved in the laboratory. The tables are turned once again. Many hold on to their newly won reality of the second phase, and fear the new realization.

Twentieth-century man is presently somewhere between the second and third phase of this second developmental stage of consciousness. We have now reached the point where the world has become completely despiritualized for us. Everything can and must have a rational explanation. What is not demonstrable is nonexistent and totally inconsequential. The second stage of the development of consciousness has successfully been entered and nears completion. The distinction between subject and object has been made to the point where God or spirit, or whatever else one would name the inexplicable cause and purpose of the universe, is no longer found in the world. Only now does science begin to realize that the energy invested in the projection of the archetypes onto the world prior to the eighteenth century by individuals, when forced out of the world by the findings of science, did not cease to exist. In fact, scientists themselves have stated that energy cannot be destroyed. That the archetypes projected out onto the world in the form of gods and spirits were "explained away" by science does not mean that the archetypes *themselves* are no longer functional.

With the advent of the sciences, a despiritualization of the world occurred—that is, the forces in nature were discovered to be laws of a logical order and not the actions of gods and spirits. Phenomena that had held mankind in awe and fear for centuries were made understandable by science. Solar eclipses, volcanic eruptions, tidal waves, thunder and lightning —"natural" forces, as opposed to supernatural events, no longer posed a mystery.

To recapitulate: The basic components of the human psyche are the archetypes, which are *forms* of knowledge. In the same manner that the form of the body (the skeletal frame and nervous system) is transmitted, so too are these forms. The manner in which they transmit their information is by the formation of images. In order to see the importance of their operations, we will now have to consider the field of their action, the human psyche.

II

If nothing else, the psyche is a self-regulating system, one which attempts to maintain a balance in itself. Approaching it with a purely mechanistic attitude, we are forced to admit that even as a manmade machine has systems which prevent it from overloading, so too does the psyche with its dreams and nervous disorders. In recent tests of dream deprivation this fact has been borne out in full.

Experiments in dream deprivation revealed that the average person dreams about twenty percent of the time he spends sleeping. After a short dream-deprivation period, the dream mechanism attempts to "make up" for lost time by spending 40 to 50 percent of the remaining sleeping time on dreaming. Dream deprivation over an extended period of time led subjects to exhibit psychotic behavior during their waking hours. Researchers are not yet sure why this is so, but their most conclusive finding is that there is a physiological *need* for humans to dream—to *dream*, not just to sleep, for the subjects were only awakened when the electroencephalograph pattern indicated a dream cycle was being entered, and were allowed to sleep the number of hours to which they were accustomed.

Mechanistically speaking, therefore, in order for the regulatory function of psyche or mind to act as a balancing and corrective agent, it must express itself in images. Behind every dream image, every vision or hallucination, every pattern of social behavior, there stands an archetype from which the basic outline of images and symbols is taken. Because the archetypes are pictorial representations of psychic energy, every symbol, inasmuch as it is produced by the archetypes, is a monad of energy. These images must be seen as monads of energy potentially available to the individual experiencing them. The energy becomes available through the individual's successful attempt at deciphering them.

Of course, this psychic mechanism has been operative as long as man has been around, its operations becoming more sophisticated and developed with the growth of consciousness. In his earlier and so-called primitive phase man did not make a distinction between subject and object. The sophistication of the psychic system occurred with the development of consciousness, which in turn was dependent on the distinctions made by the subject-object relationship.

If we pause to consider that much of our present-day knowledge is of the sort that explains the why and how of natural phenomena which cannot be discovered by experience alone, we will realize that what we call knowledge is but an acquired accumulation of statistics. But man does not himself contain this acquired information as an inherent birthright. Acquired information is the subject of personal memory, which in turn is a phenomenon of personality. If a child born in the twentieth century were never taught this information, if he were left to experience the world as is, he too would probably arrive at a naturalistic and religious cosmogony such as ancient civilizations developed.

The acquired information or knowledge accumulated throughout the ages has in so many instances become a commonplace that man too often forgets that such knowledge is an addition to his psychic system and not an original structure or component. We would do well to recall Shao Yung's statement: "Learning is an ability of man's, but our nature comes from Heaven. That nature grows from within, while learning comes to us from without." The original structure or essence of mind is the psychic mechanism that, though forgotten, is nonetheless operative behind and beneath the addition of accumulated knowledge.

Because the psyche is a system, a "mechanism" of sorts, it has lineaments, a beginning and an end, a process and an order. This then is the "natural" knowledge of the human organism. The knowledge or information natural to man— knowledge that can in no way be compared with the acquired knowledge of scientific and objective investigations into the nature of phenomena—"unacquired" knowledge, is the operation of his own psychic system. To rediscover this system it would be necessary to follow the technique suggested by Chang Tsai of working "back towards that which is hidden, and when a physical form is not present . . . [working] back towards the cause of the thing manifested."

Let us elucidate: If we forget the scientific fact that the earth revolves around the sun and observe its actions the way early man was forced to, our immediate observation would be that the sun most probably circles the earth. Even then this would be a sophisticated observation based on the knowledge that the earth is round. If we did not also have that knowledge, we would be in the position of experiencing the sun's rise and fall over and under the horizon line. We would then have to postulate what was beneath the horizon.

To begin with, the sun's passage across the sky and its descent would eventually be understood as symbolic of its birth and death. Observing that it set in the west and rose in the east, we would have to say that during its absence at night it journeyed beneath us in order to arrive back in the east. Because it was understood as having died at sunset, the land it traveled through before its new emergence would be understood as being the land of the dead, the underworld.

For ancient man, night was a painful experience, primarily because of the absence of light and warmth. The experience was heightened by the belief that with the extinction of light the dead spirits of the underworld could gain entry into the world of the living. The sun was greeted with great fervor every morning, because it had again survived its passage through the underworld, and by so doing had saved man from the nightly invasion of dark spirits. The sun was supreme, a king who daily saved man from darkness and terror.

Man in time came to see his own death as a passage through the underworld and eventual rebirth. It is for this reason that many ancient burial customs centered around the inclusions of vehicles or beasts of burden to insure the deceased a swift and certain journey through the underworld. By the same token, all attempts at preserving the body, whether the mummification techniques of the Egyptians or the modern concern with concrete-lined graves to insure against defilement of the deceased by either insects or the phenomena of soil, speak of this archetypal theme of rebirth.

From the above, we might say we have possibly viewed how there came into being the concept of death as being but a transitional phase into a new life, or the concept of rebirth. Death became synonymous with the extinction of light; birth, with the appearance of light.

Whenever the human organism attained and retained the specific form we know today, the psyche must also have attained its specific form and function. Already contained within it, the course of psychic elements that would die and be reborn existed in potential. That is, the death and birth of psychic energy—as we witness it in going to sleep and awakening—was an already established fact. Only the form, the image which would symbolize the event, was missing.

The psyche composed its grammar from the original primitive's experience of nature. Those processes that appeared to take place in nature, and that corresponded with the functioning of the psyche, became fixed at that time and came to symbolize the psyche's processes. Until this day, in all mystical and religious experiences, as well as in the dreams and visions of what one would call the common man, light symbolizes an awakening, a realization, an enlightenment, a birth of new ideas or awareness. This light symbolism, this archetype of birth, became fixed in the psyche in much the same way as the information of maze-running in the flatworm did. Of course, the archetype does not still today necessarily express itself as the sun. Because of our experience of the world, the archetype may present itself in dreams and visions as artificial or electric light. Nevertheless, the form expressed is still that of light.

We still carry the original essence of mind within us. It stands behind the acquired structure of consciousness we too often believe to be the final judge and guide. It is only through the original psychic structure that transformation is possible. It is therefore essential that one learn to discriminate between the original and the acquired psychic structure. Before entering the Way it is necessary to first separate and divide. We must reach a position where we can discriminate between what is truly ourselves and what is the collective man we carry. This is not to say we should discredit the acquired system, but that we should recognize it as being *acquired*, and therefore but a subsidiary limb that enables us to function in the mainstream of the world, to move with ease in the reality we have spun out of our own bodies. But of the other reality, that which truly shapes us and determines whether our journey through this world has been one in which the fullest expression of the creativity we are each capable of has been fulfilled, there is still much to learn and discover.

A temporary suspension of the acquired structure, that is, a lowering of consciousness, is often necessary to penetrate this deeper realm; but this is a dangerous enterprise, one which few individuals are capable of surviving. We are not all mystics. True spiritual or psychological transformation (choose whichever phrase sits easier with you, they mean the same) is a must if life is to be meaningful, but it appears that there are a limited number of methods available for the majority of Westerners.

Many of us have mistaken the way of certain Near Eastern and Eastern disciplines that demand a dissolution of ego to be the only way transformation is feasible. This is a great error. The Near Easterner and Easterner have a tradition of spiritual unity that supports the individual in his quest. De-egoized personalities not only have a function and place set aside for them in society, they are also allowed to be instrumental in directing their society. When they become one with the original unity, they also become one with their society, for their society is understood as being patterned after the divine order. To lose one's ego is to lose one's orientation in the world. But if the world is understood as being but a model of the transcendent realm, how then can one be disoriented? Such is the way of the Oriental.

It is the tragic and mistaken belief of many in America that what is needed is a destruction of ego, a burning away of that component of personality that is called "me." It is those proponents of Eastern philosophy, those who in typical Occidental fashion have investigated the truth of the Orient's valid

religious intuitions with their intellect and with their where-
there-is-a-will-there-is-a-way attitude, rather than with their
hearts, whom we must thank for this graceless state of affairs.
Any investigation into being that is not totally committed to
the support and reconstitution of what by its very nature is a
part of the world, if not the world itself, must be defined as
irreligious and disrespectful of spirit.

That the Occidental must seek support and comfort in systems foreign to himself is an indication that his ego is *underdeveloped,* not overdeveloped as we too often assume. Because a person is egotistical does not mean he has a strong
ego. On the contrary, it is an indication that deep down inside the personality is so unsure of itself that it must build up
defenses against the world, construct walls of superficial
values, and maintain, at all costs, that it is on top of the
world. That many Americans now lean toward Oriental ideas
is an admission that we do not in fact know it all. But that is
all the more reason to proceed with caution.

An underdeveloped ego needs strengthening. One cannot
tear down and reassemble what he does not have. The Oriental's method of tearing down, burning away, and denying of
ego has to do with the fact that he *has* something to
work with and to rework. His is a problem of stripping himself of an excess of ego. Even the medieval alchemists knew
that in order to make gold they had to begin the process with
something, even if it was a base metal. Because they often
said one must start with lead, one of the heaviest substances
in the world, we may infer that we are to begin the process of
transformation with that which is substantial, if not heavy to
the point of its being unbearable.

We may safely define ego as that substance of being that
comes into existence, and gains in substance and form,
through an active participation in the world—through making real one's wishes and desires. The Taoist's statement that
one should seek action in nonaction does not mean a dissolution of personality, but rather that the personality should
allow things to happen, through an acceptance and awareness
of what one is, no matter how painful the realization might
be.

If we in the West are truly to have a spiritual life again, it
must be founded on the experience of Western man. It is not
enough to reap the harvest of another's suffering, to adopt

forms of religious and mystical practice developed out of historical precedents of little import to our own development. Out of his awareness and concern over his specific suffering, the spiritual Oriental has come to peace with the conflicting elements of his world. The Occidental, however, has experienced and is still experiencing incomparable pain and suffering without the benefit of understanding its cause and meaning.

The Oriental's vision grew out of his investigation of the cause of his own pain, not that of others in other countries. The value and substance of his method is a direct result of his constant refusal to look beyond himself and his predicament. We in the West too easily adapt ourselves to forms of altruistic living whose roots, if we should seek them, could not properly be implanted in us. That foreign systems of spiritual transformation do have substance, that they do transform and are enlightened forms of knowledge, goes without saying. But what must be transformed are roots.

The spiritual life is a responsible life—one that calls upon the individual not only to save himself but by so doing to affect others to the degree that they themselves seek and devise new and significant forms of transformation. Many of us today follow Eastern forms, but practically all ignore the message of the Buddha's action: He realized that his achievement, his new awareness, was of little import if he restricted himself to the life of a hermit. He came down off his mountain. It is time we leveled ours.

Because of what happened in the West during the seventeenth and eighteenth centuries—the commencement of the despiritualization of the world—we in the West do not have a spiritual tradition of any sort. The Oriental remains centered through a close contact with nature or with a society that imitates a transcendent order. Therefore, we cannot borrow existing forms of transformation from the Orient. We can only use them as models from which we might construct our own Way. The Westerner must rediscover the spiritual dimension that is uniquely his. Western man has little contact with the reality that contains him and he lacks a spiritual tradition; therefore, to lose his ego is to find himself adrift in the cosmos. Although union with the cosmos, or with that deepest layer of our being, is a centering, a being in Tao, to be set adrift is to be unmoored, decentered. Whatever support the Westerner is to find in his new adventure must be found within himself.

We are therefore fortunate that many who have entered that realm of original psyche left behind traces, records of the experience. These records in time became systems, or methods of transformation. Such systems stand between the individual and the powerful energies residing in that dimension, thereby shielding him from the full blast of the cosmos. The geography of that other dimension has been mapped countless times throughout the history of the world and may be found in the mystical, magical, and religious texts of mankind. Even now, in the mind of science, the survey continues. In short, we have discovered the underground in ourselves and now are busy mapping it from this newly acquired vantage point.

Now we know that the energy we discovered in the world is actually contained within us, and we slowly begin to recognize that this energy is capable of transforming the individual. Whatever function we believe this energy to have, whether we accept the theories of Freud, Adler, Jung, or Reich, we now accept the premise that there is a force contained within each of us that resides outside the immediate range of consciousness and strives to express itself within the scope of its purpose—transformation. Man's task is to find and let this spirit express itself naturally. Recognition of this principle is the first step; a dialogue with it is the second; a successful integration of it into our daily experiences is the third, and final step. But because twentieth-century man is so cut off from that original experience of mind, he must rely on the recorded systems that have been born out of this original experience. I do not here attempt to promote a return to primitivism, but rather to foster an acknowledgment of that portion of our being that is operative whether we are conscious of it or not. To become aware of its existence is to become aware of the true reality in which we are contained.

III

What makes the *I Ching* unique is that it speaks the pure language of archetypes. Created by Orientals, it is in no way Oriental. Its images—the trigrams and hexagrams—are only symbols of the original psychic structure common to all of mankind. Of all instruments of transformation it is in my estimation the best for it deals in simple language directly with the situation at hand.

Many will wonder at the wisdom of presenting to the general public what purports to be a system that in many ways demands that the individual turn to and activate the deepest stratum of his being, because when one releases the powers of the unconscious, or whatever else one might call that other dimension, it is difficult to shut the door again. Any investigation into being is an heroic and therefore dangerous journey. At another time in history it might have been difficult to justify the creation of this book, but now, in the twentieth century, there is little need for justification. That other realm of experience has already been activated, has already forced man into a position where he must confront himself and question the wisdom of his actions. Having ignored that other dimension for so long a period of time, we now find ourselves faced with its insistence that we recognize its existence, its insistence that we give it its place in the world and in ourselves. The widespread use of mind-expanding drugs in this century is symptomatic of man's basic need and desire to experience that other dimension. Whether the employment of drugs is a proper course of action is beside the point.

Because we have repressed and ignored the spirit for so long a time, it cares little what effect it has. In its driving insistence to emerge, it seems to have affected man and his world negatively. It now lends itself to violence and tyranny. Because the dangerous aspects of the unconscious already race through the world, there is every reason for the Westerner to investigate methods by which he may counter its effects, ways in which he may contain this spirit and benefit from its great energy. The *I Ching,* in every respect, appears to be capable of fulfilling this need.

Chapter 1

FIRST PRINCIPLES

I

The roots of the *I Ching* reach far back in time—as far back as the twelfth century B.C. The *I Ching* confronts us with the careful observations and considerations of men who sought to record the meaningful relationships existing between man, nature, and the universe. Foremost in their investigations was the theory of the opposites, or yin and yang, and the effects of their commingling in time and space.

Presently understood as philosophical terms for the two aspects of an original unity and force, the terms yin and yang originated out of the meteorological observations of peasants, which in time became the rudiments of a folk psychology. The concept of the opposites is truly an indigenous product of Chinese thought.

These two forces cannot exist independently. They support one another. Yang (the male force) begins things, impregnates things with its pure spirit-substance; yin completes what was begun by yang, gives it the form and substance without which the male force would become dissipated.

When Tai Chi, the original unity or supreme ultimate, moves toward differentiation, it splits in half, the halves being the yin and yang. The two forces when mingling with one another as husband and wife give birth to the four emblems, or elements, and the elements in turn give birth to the eight trigrams, which are understood as representing the world.

In the beginning, the ideograms for yin and yang stood for sunshine and the absence of sunshine on a mountain. Yang was the south and sunny side, yin the north and shadowy side. Of the many significations given them the following were the most important: male (yang), female (yin); heaven (yang), earth (yin); above (yang), below (yin); anterior (yang), posterior (yin); hard (yang), soft (yin); light (yang), heavy (yin).

19

Originally, yin and yang were understood to be forces operating in nature, affecting and motivating things by their interaction with one another. They themselves were in no way affected. However, when introduced to the divinatory structure of the *I Ching,* they became influenced by each other to such a degree that they changed into one another. It was no longer a simple matter of give and take, but an approaching, a merging, and a transformation.

To record this event the framers of the *I Ching* elected to identify the yang and masculine principle by an unbroken line (————); the yin and feminine, by a broken line (—— ——). In addition, numerical values were assigned them: a yang line could have a value of 7 or 9; a yin, 6 or 8. Putting aside for the moment the magical and religious reasoning behind these numbers, they were the means by which the diviner determined which principle, the yin or the yang, and in what combination with its opposite, was operative in any particular moment in time. To illustrate how this was done we will here outline the most popular and modern method of *I Ching* divination—the coin-oracle method.

Assigning a numerical value of 2 to the heads side of a coin, 3 to the tails side, one throws three coins simultaneously, to receive a sum of either 6, 7, 8, or 9. That is, three heads would yield a yin line with the value of 6; two heads and a tail, a yang line with a value of 7; one head and two tails, a yin line with a value of 8; three tails, a yang line with a value of 9. Lines with a numerical value of 6 or 9 are carefully distinguished from those with a value of 7 or 8 because they are moving or changing lines. That is, a yin line with a value of 6 changes into its opposite, a yang line with a value of 7; a yang line with a value of 9, into a yin line with a value of 8. The entire notational system looks like this:*

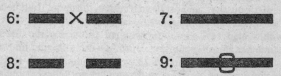

---

* The X assigned the broken line and the O assigned the unbroken line are traditional notations for *changing* yin and yang lines respectively.

Throwing three coins six times leaves one with one of the sixty-four hexagrams composing the *I Ching*. Any time one throws a hexagram containing one or more of either changing lines (6 or 9), a second hexagram comes into existence.

For example: if one were to throw the following hexa-

(Hexagram 57)

gram, by virtue of the fact that 6's and 9's change into their opposites, one would then need to draw the resulting hexagram it "changes" into:

(Hexagram 60)

With these two hexagrams before him, he would then read the text assigned the original or thrown hexagram, concluding his reading with the second or derived one. In reading the first hexagram he would not only read the text that gives a general discussion of the hexagram in question, but because of the added significance given the lines with values of 6 and 9, would also read the text assigned those specific lines. In our first hexagram, counting from the bottom up, he would read the textual comments for lines one, three, and six. Changing lines either modify or amplify the general meaning of the hexagram they are contained in and are for that reason particularly significant in the answer received by the inquirer. Having read these lines, the inquirer would then turn to the hexagram the first changed into. This derived or changed

hexagram further elucidates the situation referred to in the
first hexagram or, in the case where the first hexagram speaks
of a dilemma, suggests a new and proper course of action.

The next question that comes to mind is how and why this
notation system of broken and unbroken lines and their numerical values came into existence. In tracing the history of
this event, we will also reconstruct the history of the *I
Ching*'s creation, keeping in mind that its dynamic components crystallize as independent systems long before they
merge into the book's framework.

II

In reading Chinese historical records we find that sometime
during the fourth century B.C. there existed two other texts
similar in construction to the *I Ching*. All that remains of
these texts are their titles: *Lien Shan*—"Manifestation of
Change in the Mountains"—and *Kuei Ts'ang*—"Flow and
Return to Womb and Tomb." These, along with the *I Ching*,
were the responsibility of the grand augur of the imperial
court. Because the Chinese firmly believed that the success of
government depended solely on an alignment of society, in all
of its ramifications, with the unimpeachable order inherent in
nature and the universe, divinatory methods were a matter of
daily course in court life. Observation of natural phenomena
was not enough. A direct and open line with supernatural
powers had to be maintained. Divination and the creation of
divinatory texts was a serious matter.

One of the earliest and most frequently used forms was
tortoise-shell divination, first mentioned in the annals of the
Shang dynasty (1520–1030 B.C.). The diviner applied a
heated metal rod to the carapace of a tortoise, causing cracks
to be formed that he then "read," or interpreted. The results
of these readings were carefully recorded and, in fact, consti-
tute the earliest historical records of the Chinese. But no-
where do we find how these crack configurations were deciphered. Obviously, the method was either part of a secret
oral tradition, or, owing to the limitless number of configurations that could be achieved by the method, too difficult and
confusing to record. Because the Oriental was so meticulous
a recordkeeper, and because we find no record of the method
of interpretation, we may assume the latter to have been the

case. Obviously, the court diviners must have wanted to limit the possible number of configurations, if not to replace them with signs of a simple, recognizable, and fixed nature. As we shall see, the notation system of broken and unbroken lines was patterned after these crack configurations.

In the meantime, in a text of 645 B.C., we find the following statement: "The tortoise-shell has its emblems [configurations], the milfoil its numbers." Milfoil, or yarrow-stalk, divination, began to be used in conjunction with the older divinatory form, possibly as an aid or means of checking it. The reference to numbers implies that a numerology of mystical proportion, somewhat akin to Pythagorean theory, was in existence. The section of the *I Ching* that tells us of this method reads, "They [the yarrow stalks] are counted through by fours, to represent the four seasons. The remainder is put aside to represent the intercalary month." The implication here is that the numerical categories employed in yarrow-stalk divination had to do with the numbers derived from the operations of natural phenomena throughout the course of the year. This correspondence between number and nature grew out of the Oriental's involvement with calendar making, an involvement that dates back as far as the sixteenth century B.C.

Up to this point we have traced the development of two important elements of the *I Ching*. Sometime during the fourth century B.C., by combining the simplest form of tortoise-shell crack configuration (a broken and unbroken line) with the traditional yin and yang system, a diviner made a simple but highly efficient and symbolically charged notation system. The many configurations caused to form on the carapace of the tortoise were in this manner simplified and given the fixed forms we now know as hexagrams. To this he added the number symbolism of the yarrow stalks, using the stalks themselves to tap the universe for information.

Therefore, the precursor of the *I Ching* we have today contained the following: a simple notation system of broken and unbroken lines to record information; a highly developed theory of the opposites with its manifold associations exemplified by the lines; an equally intricate and mystical number symbolism, also merged with the lines; sixty-four fixed, oracular figures within which the above three elements fluctuated, yielding still further levels of meaning; and finally, in the yarrow stalks, a simplified method for receiving one of the sixty-four hexagrams in answer to a question.

The complicated and lengthy method of tortoise-shell divination was soon to become a thing of the past, but not before the last and most important element of the book was added —the text.

By the year 7 B.C. a great number of compilations containing the accumulated observations of Chinese farmers and commonfolk existed. They were really the observations of everyday occurrences mingled with what we would today call superstitious omens. A few examples from the *I Ching* are as follows: "Cockcrow penetrating to heaven. Perseverance brings misfortune." "Return from a short distance. No need for remorse. Great good fortune." "One does not drink the mud of the well. No animals come to an old well."

These and other such omens were lifted out of the peasant texts and assigned to each line of the sixty-four hexagrams.

The basic structure of the *I Ching* is now complete. True, in this form it is little more than a fortune-telling device. If it were not for the philosophical and ethical speculations appended to the book by Confucian and Taoist philosophers between 3 B.C. and 3 A.D., the book would not have been preserved. The application of philosophical superstructures to the lines and hexagrams stripped the book of its superstitious qualities. Such lines as "One should cross the great water," took on metaphysical and spiritual proportions, causing the reader to discover where in himself the great water existed and what aspect of his personality it was that he must cross over, i.e., change or revise. There were various reasons for the philosophers' bothering with a divinatory text. For our purposes all that need be known is that they recognized in it the workings of the Tao.

The word *Tao* originally meant a road or way, and was metaphorically understood as standing for the Way of man, his morality and conduct in society. At least this was the view rigorously maintained by the Confucians. The Tao to them meant the source of morality and ethics. The Taoists, on the other hand, insisted that the Tao spoke of the necessity of aligning oneself not with the laws of human society, but with the laws of nature and the universe. True understanding and morality were not to be achieved by religiously following the laws of society and government, but by intuitively recognizing the correct way of doing things, or even of not doing them. The Taoists were also the first to make of the Tao a metaphysical formulation: the first principle out of which the universe was created. In time, this concept was further developed to include a theory of mind wherein the Tao was understood to be the active principle of consciousness.

Regardless of their differences, both the Taoist and the Confucian understood the Tao to be a unity that in some mysterious fashion served man as a guideline in his life. In addition, they were both faced with the problem of defining the particulars of this unity so that they might actively be put into practice. The two schools eventually agreed that the order or law of the Tao was visibly operative in the interplay of the opposites, both understanding that when things reach their fullest potential they revert to their opposite. Because of this, all things—and man—were viewed as being in a constant state of flux. It was therefore important to both schools to discover the middle way, to devise a method by which the opposites of mind and body might be balanced and united. They both believed that the *I Ching* supplied the method and therefore both schools contributed heavily to the philosophical structure of the book.

Miraculously, time did something neither school would have thought possible. The ethical formulations of the Confucians and the metaphysical speculation of the Taoists became comfortably united within the framework of the book they each claimed as their own. The *I Ching,* therefore, is as unified as the original unity, the Tao, it exemplifies. It is essentially a book of guidance, for its function is to reveal to the individual the correctness or the incorrectness of his life, attitudes, desires, or predicaments. It is an instrument of transformation in that it attempts to align the individual with the original unity composed of both the ethical and metaphysical realms, thereby making of his life a perpetual unfolding and reintegration with the forces that at every moment affect him. As far as this is true, the *I Ching is* the Tao.

Chapter 2

THE HEXAGRAM
PART I

Internal Components

The sixty-four six-lined figures composing the *Book of Changes* are known as hexagrams. The lines of a hexagram are visualized as entering the figure from below and moving upward. That is, the first line of a hexagram is its botom line; the sixth and last, the top line.

Each hexagram must be understood as being a symbol outlining not only the dimensions of a specific situation or time, but containing the antecedents that caused it to come into existence, as well as all its possible future aspects. To understand the dynamics of a hexagram it is necessary to realize that a symbol is not simply a design or pattern by which something else is identified.

The symbol is a dynamic and living entity itself, the bearer of information important for the process of transformation that is constantly going on in both the race and individual psyche. On the one hand, the symbol is a product of the psyche; on the other, it is the very thing that constantly shapes and directs the psyche. It is at one and the same time parent and child. It is a *function* of mind. The symbol *always* contains information that has not yet reached the conscious awareness of the race or the individual. The information is experienced as energy, as effects, awe, aesthetic pleasure, fear, etc., thought of as coming *from* the symbol. Sometimes just the experience of receiving this information is capable of sustaining its effect throughout the course of an individual's life, lending it a substance and meaning beyond the often futile and meaningless contrivances devised by the ego. But here I speak of those instances where the symbol becomes benevolently deified. Deification does not necessarily guarantee that the symbol's present manifestation will be a benevolent one. The swastika for many centuries was revered as the sun, father, and protector of all; but in the twentieth century it came to represent a black, burning sun, destructive and evil. However, the point to be made here is that the spiritual quality of the symbol itself, its energy, is operative regardless of whether its emergence means good or evil. The important thing to take note of is the fact that the symbol contains power, energy, and information capable of rallying great numbers around it. Because of the symbol's magnetic power, it is important that modern man learn the grammar of symbols—and thereby learn to relate to and make compensation for the information the symbol contains.

Because the symbol is a function of the psyche and has its origins in the psyche, it is obvious that its effect does not come from the symbol as it exists in outer reality—as a painting, poem, or religious object, for example—but from within the individual. The affect is pure psychic energy and, because energy reveals itself as an agent of transformation when expressed as a symbol, all attempts must be made to understand its functioning in the personality.

(I write these words only two days before man's planned walk on the moon [August, 1969] and while writing wonder if the collective psyche during the remaining years of this century will not be radically affected by this event in a way never experienced before. I say this because the moon over the entire course of man's history has always been invested with a considerable amount of psychic energy, enough to have become one of the most important symbols of mankind. Now that this hitherto inaccessible orb will soon be within man's grasp, much if not all of its symbolic value will be lost. As Jung pointed out, it is in what is unknown that we invest most of our energy. Now that the moon is attained physically and known intimately, where will the energy we used to devote to it next manifest itself, and will its reemergence be of a positive or of a negative nature?)

In each hexagram we have a symbol: the hexagram itself. The hexagram often speaks to us simply, through our intuitive faculty, giving us information and answers whose meaning can rarely be expressed rationally. What the symbol speaks to is the heart.

In the *Great Commentary* (*Ta Chuan*) appended to the *Book of Changes,* we are told that objects or things are distinguished from one another by being assigned to definite classes. Each hexagram is thought of as a symbol standing for

more than one class of things. The Confucian rectification of
names is operative here. This is an ancient philosophical concept that holds that the name of an object is its essence. The
object's name reveals not only its function, but its special
characteristics. A bread knife is that and nothing more. Its
proper use is the cutting of bread; it is definitely not a carv-
ing, butter, or cheese knife. That a bread knife and a butter
knife are both used to cut is the distinction of the larger class
they are both contained in, the class of "knife." The rectification of names demands that it be understood that the function of a knife is to cut, and nothing more. Therefore, both
bread knife and butter knife are properly employed when
they are used to cut; but the bread knife should cut bread,
the butter knife, butter.

The Confucian rectification of names might appear to be a
matter of little consequence for the major problems and ideas
of Chinese philosophy. However, when one considers that
during the period Confucius called for the rectification of
names—the assigning of things to their class and true function—the Chinese were in a state of constant war. All but the
aristocracy were oppressed, and even they did not escape tor-
ture and death. Life was of little value and few if any distinctions were made between right and wrong, good and evil.
Previously, rulers had been revered as protectors and guides;
now they were considered tyrants and thieves, pillagers of the
land and people. That the Confucian ethic had to call upon
the rulers to act as rulers, fathers to act as fathers, sons as
sons, is indication enough that humanity and righteousness
had become displaced by the indiscriminate and selfish desires of men without conscience

Understanding the justification for the rectification of
names during such a period is not, however, enough to reveal
its relevance in *I Ching* interpretation. In order to find the
value of this ancient doctrine that is pertinent to our discussion, it is first necessary to discover its meaning within the
framework of the archetypal dimension referred to earlier in
this book—the dimension that gives further substance to the
tangible and mundane reality we all commonly experience.

In every story of the creation of the world, there comes the
moment of naming, or the time of distinctions. This moment
always immediately follows the decision to create order out
of chaos and it is always one that demands, on the one hand,

self-awareness and, therefore, on the other, the distinction between subject and object, and among classes of objects. In the
account of the creation in the Old Testament, Adam is called
upon to give names to the animals; in the Tantric creation
story the moment of self-awareness is emphasized by God's
sudden realization that he *is*. In both cases, the discriminating
quality comes into existence with the naming of an object or
objects, and their classification. In many religious and magical practices, it is the name of the object or deity that contains power. The most fully developed system basing its dynamics on this name-or-word-as-power theory is found in the
Hindu practice of mantra recitation. A mantra, simply defined, is a collection of words or syllables containing the
power of the deity.

In attempting to bring order out of the confusion and
chaos of his time by a rectification of names, Confucius was
motivated by the same principle of the archetype that eternally stands behind the creative process. This is regardless of
whether that process is understood as taking place within a
transpersonal time and place, or as operating in the mundane
and subjective world. Because creativity is essentially that
process by which one produces unity from elements seemingly too diverse in form, function, and character ever to be
reconciled with one other, the concept behind the rectification of names is one that can be immediately applicable in
personality transformation.

The *Great Commentary* tells us, "The *Book of Changes*
contains heaven and earth's measure"; that is, each class,
each one of the sixty-four hexagrams, reveals the proper
course of action that will eventually lead to man's coming "to
resemble heaven and earth." The *Great Commentary* goes on
to tell us that this is achieved because one is no longer in
conflict with heaven and earth, no longer tossed about by the
conflict of the opposites. When man finds the measure of
heaven and earth within himself—the measure of *his own
heaven and earth*—the conflict is nullified by their marriage
and peaceful union. This is the keystone of the book's message, its hidden touchstone capable of turning all things to
gold.

The hexagram must be understood as representative of a
class of objects. Although each hexagram specifically refers
us to a class, each object in that class is not equal to any

other object in the same class. For example, Hexagram 48 refers us to the idea of a well—the *idea,* not the object itself. It uses the image of a well because the well's use, function, and condition best represent the archetypal principle to which the hexagram refers. In this instance, the idea is of a container within which something of great value is stored. The container within which all actions and decisions are significant can in no way be equal to an occupation thought of as container, for in the latter all of life's decisions or actions are not pertinent, just those that specifically belong in that "container." Hence, each object in the class of well is not equal to every other object in that class. Moreover, some objects in the class are closer to the idea the hexagram speaks of than some others which are peripheral.

The condition or state exemplified by the hexagram is of a generalized nature; it refers us to the principle underlying all the objects related to that class. When we are in the presence of a changing line, a moment of emphasis, the general statement of the hexagram is affected. The hexagram in its totality might refer us to a positive state of affairs, but an unfavorable line modifies the meaning. In Hexagram 24, Return, the general prognosis is favorable, but line six tells us that during the time of return, we have missed the mark. In Hexagram 38, Opposition, the prognosis is generally unfavorable. However, in line three, we are told that although there has not been a good beginning, there will be a good end. At least one of the lines of each hexagram will come close to contradicting the general statement of the hexagram, thereby highlighting one object of the class.

What each hexagram refers us to is the underlying principle, the Tao, of the class. For example, in Hexagram 18, Work on What Has Been Spoiled, when it is said that what must be worked on is that which has been spoiled by the mother, the hexagram is not necessarily speaking of one's mother, but rather of the motherly quality of the yin principle. Decay has come about because the reticent nature of the yin principle has been too much in the forefront of one's activities. The underlying principle, or Tao, of this line, is the quiescent nature of the yin; the Tao of the hexagram, on the other hand, is that of balancing, of setting right the under- or overemphasis of the yin and yang, working on what has been spoiled by them.

Another section of the *Great Commentary* sheds further light:

> Circumstances follow distinct tendencies, each in accordance with its nature. All things are made distinct from one another by the definitiveness of their classes . . . Phenomena take form in heaven; shapes take form on earth.

The first two sentences refer to what has just been discussed above. It is the last sentence that now interests us. The phenomena referred to here are those of the archetypal realm, heaven—that place where the archetypes take form. The shapes that take form on earth are patterned after those archetypal phenomena. Each hexagram is a symbolic pictogram of one of those phenomena or archetypes, of which, according to the cosmogony of the *I Ching*, there are sixty-four. As the *Great Commentary* states, "The sages created the hexagrams so that we might see in them phenomena." The *Book of Changes* is the only book of its kind; it contains the field of the archetypal realm in its entirety.

There are two major divisions to a hexagram: the two trigrams and the three places. The trigrams, which will be discussed in detail in chapter 5, are of the utmost importance; the three places, although referred to only in the *I Ching*'s appendices, are also significant, as we shall soon see. Let us first briefly discuss the trigrams as qualities of the hexagram.

I. *The Trigram as Hexagram Component*

Regarded solely as components of a hexagram, the two trigrams composing it must be understood as expressions of the hexagram's antithetical nature. They are referred to as primary trigrams in order to distinguish them from the nuclear trigrams to be discussed below:

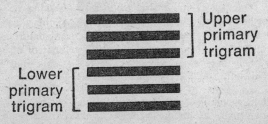

] Upper primary trigram

Lower primary trigram [

Here too, in the structure of the hexagram, the nature of the opposites is expressed. The upper three lines of a hexagram, the fourth, fifth, and sixth lines, represent that which is above, in front of, in the future; the lower three lines, the first, second, and third lines, represent that which is below, in back of, in the past.

A hexagram that portrays the antithesis of behind of and in front of is Hexagram 39, Obstruction.

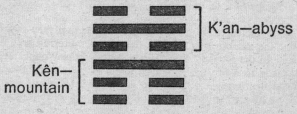

The picture is of an abyss (upper trigram, K'an) before one and a steep mountain (the lower trigram, Kên) behind one. Hexagram 36, Darkening of the Light, shows us a sun (lower trigram, Li) hidden beneath the earth (lower trigram, K'un).

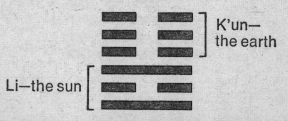

Often, when one has a changing line in the lower and upper trigram, the line in the lower trigram refers us to what is in the past, the line in the upper, what is in the present or future.

II. *The Nuclear Trigram*

The second, third, and fourth lines, along with the third, fourth, and fifth lines compose the two nuclear trigrams of a hexagram. The trigram made up of the second, third, and fourth lines is referred to as the lower nuclear trigram; the third, fourth, and fifth lines, the upper nuclear trigram.

The nuclear trigrams are important because they often reveal the reason why certain objects are referred to in the lines. In the second line of Hexagram 48, The Well, reference is made to a broken jug. In looking at the significations for the two primary trigrams, K'an and Sun, we find the signification of jug assigned to neither one. However, in looking up the significations for the upper nuclear trigram, Li, we find that it represents a jug.

Knowing that the lower primary trigram, Sun, also has as one of its significations the act of breaking, we therefore arrive at the image of a broken jug. When we discuss the trigrams in Chapter 5, we will discover that each trigram has a specific movement. The pushing upward of Hexagram 46 will then be understood as an activity caused by the upper nuclear tri-

gram, Chen, its movement understood as an upward movement. It is with the aid of the nuclear trigrams that one eventually sees the pictures of the hexagrams; sometimes one recognizes the nature of the hexagram before referring to the *I
Ching* itself.

III. *The Nuclear Hexagrams*

In all there are five nuclear hexagrams to a hexagram.
They are distinguished as follows:

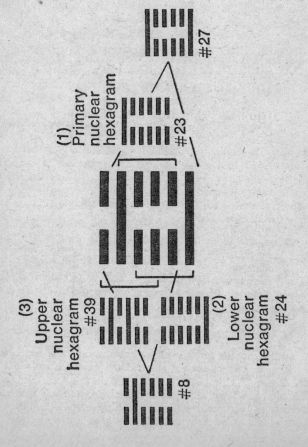

Before showing the value of these nuclear hexagrams in understanding Hexagram 3, it is necessary to mention that their relevance may not be as immediately discernible as they appear in this hexagram. The nature of the question itself often determines whether or not any of the nuclear hexagrams are relevant at the time. Again, if the hexagram speaks to you directly, there is no need to dig further. The nuclear hexagrams often reveal either the cause of the "time" of the hexagram, or the factors actively influencing that time. The safest rule of thumb is to view the nuclear hexagram as one of the "causes" of the primary hexagram's condition. This will become clearer below.

In Hexagram 3, Difficulty at the Beginning, the first nuclear hexagram of importance is that made up of the two nuclear trigrams: the second, third, and fourth lines, and the third, fourth, and fifth lines. This first nuclear trigram is Number 23, Splitting Apart.

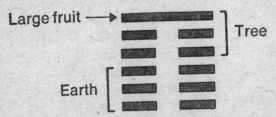

Hexagram 3 is the hexagram that speaks of the difficulties of beginnings, the difficulties of birth. What is being born is the active yang principle, the yang line in the first place, referred to as a blade of grass. The idea is that of a blade of grass pushing its way up through the earth. In the nuclear hexagram of Splitting Apart (Number 23), we discover that the yang line at the top of the hexagram is spoken of as "leaving the picture," that is, of being pushed up and out, or dislodged. Here it must be remembered that the lines of a hexagram are understood to enter the hexagram from below and exit through the top. Hence, the picture here is of five yin lines pressing upward and pushing the last remaining yang line out of the picture.

In the text accompanying this yang line it is spoken of as being a large fruit, which, when evicted from the top, falls to earth, decays, and is reborn when its seeds take root. Therefore, the birth referred to in the primary hexagram, Difficulty at the Beginning, has come about because of such an event. Here, the flux of the opposites, their coming and going, is commented upon: When a thing has reached its pinnacle, its fullest expression, it is replaced by its opposite, it must give the field over to its complement. To do this, it must not only "fall," as it were, but must also dissolve or decay. It is in this giving over of itself, in its dying and dissolution, that its rebirth and return is guaranteed. The visual statement made in this hexagram is that the difficulty of birth comes about because of the necessary assembling or reassembling of that which had in the past been dispersed. Here the yang principle has been gathered together again and is as a child in its womb, or a seedling hidden beneath the surface of the earth.

The lower nuclear hexagram, composed of the first, second, third, and the second, third, and fourth lines is Hexagram 24, Return.

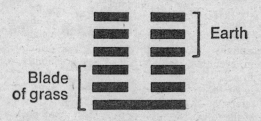

In Hexagram 24, we find that what is returning is the overthrown yang line of Hexagram 23, Splitting Apart—once again in accordance with the dynamics of the opposites. Reading Hexagram 24, we are again referred to the idea that energy cannot die, that the operations of the opposites are eternal. Another statement this nuclear hexagram seems to make is that in all returns there is difficulty; that no return, either from a short or a great distance, is without its difficulties. Hexagram 3, the primary hexagram we are discussing, shows us not only the reason that this time has come about (because of the splitting apart), but the nature and quality of the return as well.

The third nuclear hexagram is made up of the third, fourth, fifth, and fourth, fifth, and sixth lines. It is Hexagram 39, Obstruction.

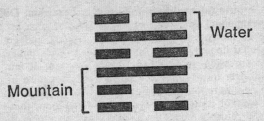

The difficulty of the birth comes about because of an obstruction. What is the nature of the obstruction? To answer this question we must again look at the second nuclear hexagram, Number 24.

In Hexagram 24 we note that the one yang line must push the five yin lines above it upward if it is to advance, in much the same way a seedling must push the earth pressing down on it up and out of its way. The statement the picture makes is that the yang principle is impeded by the oppressive heaviness and thickness of the negative expression of the yin quality: the sloth that arises out of a *too* receptive state of being. The receptivity and devotedness of the yin principle, if indulged in, eventually leads to an ineptness, inability, or plain refusal to act. The serenity of the past suddenly becomes the obstinacy of the future. The number of yin lines in this instance refers us to such an excess, and reveals not only the nature of the difficulty, but also the cause of the obstruction.

The ideogram, Chien, of Hexagram 39, Obstruction, is actually a symbol for a weakness in the feet and legs. The obstruction in this hexagram comes about because of a difficulty in walking. In Hexagram 3, this difficulty becomes the difficulty a young blade of grass encounters in attempting to advance. Again, the difficulty arises out of the excessive quiescence of the yin principle. This only applies to Hexagram 39 as the nuclear hexagram of Hexagram 3. When discussing Hexagram 39 as a primary hexagram we would not necessarily find this to be the case. The nature of Hexagram 39 in that instance would have to be defined by the nuclear trigrams it contains. Here, in Hexagram 3, it only lends its quality of obstruction to the picture.

The three nuclear hexagrams we have just discussed might be thought of as the most important of the five a hexagram contains. The reason these three nuclear hexagrams are of greater importance than the two yet to be discussed is that in each of the three either the first or last line occupies the second or fifth place of the primary hexagram—in this case, Hexagram 3. The relevance of the second and fifth places of a hexagram will be discussed when we speak of the lines of a hexagram. The other two nuclear hexagrams, it will be found, rarely shed as much light as the first three. In this particular instance, however, we shall find the fourth and fifth nuclear hexagrams to be just as significant.

The fourth nuclear hexagram is made up of the first, second, third, and third, fourth, and fifth lines. This gives us Hexagram 27, The Corners of the Mouth or The Providing of Nourishment.

The picture is of an open mouth, the first and sixth lines being the lips, the second, third, and fourth lines being the opening and teeth. Within the context of Hexagram 3, the primary hexagram we are discussing, the hexagram would appear to be saying that during the time of birth and the difficulty surrounding it, it is important that nourishment be provided, i.e., that we feed the situation, be as active as the yang principle.

The fifth nuclear hexagram is made up of the second, third, fourth, and fourth, fifth, and sixth lines. The hexagram resulting from this combination leaves us with Hexagram 8, Holding Together.

That hexagram shows us that the waters of the earth all attempt to come together at one place. Out of the innumerable rivers, comes the unity of the ocean. What is important in times of birth or beginnings is to hold together, to unite those elements that have only recently entered or reentered the picture.

We have just analyzed Hexagram 3 for the information its five nuclear hexagrams contain. In actual usage, such a detailed analysis is often not necessary. This and many other interpretive methods to be discussed in this book, is but one of many "layers" that might be peeled away from the hexagram when it does not appear to speak directly. To follow this method every time one reads a hexagram would be tedious. In time, the user of the *Book of Changes* comes to recognize the hexagrams contained within the primary hexagram and can make quick associations between the question at hand and the information of the nuclear hexagrams. Because there are so many elements to be considered when viewing a hexagram, certain of them will be of more relevance than others at any one specific time. On one day the information of a nuclear hexagram might be of particular significance, while on another the same nuclear hexagram, contained in the same primary hexagram, might be absolutely empty of meaning. All this depends on the question asked at the particular time. For this reason, the question itself is an element in hexagram interpretation that must be looked into and considered.

The problem is one of asking the question correctly. In asking a question, the individual must discriminate between what is relevant and what is irrelevant to the situation at hand. To ask a question is to admit that a portion of your landscape is missing or unknown to you. The question by its very nature states that the questioner is ignorant of something, that he is conscious of the fact that there is a missing factor that must be known before something can be resolved or understood.

For example, in the tale of Parsifal, concerning his search for the Holy Grail, Parsifal was entertained one night in a castle where, in the presence of an ill and dying king, he and others were served from a vessel whose contents never seemed to diminish no matter how many people were served. As unusual as the circumstances around him were, Parsifal at no time asked either the cause of the king's illness or the nature of the miraculous vessel. Instead, he fell asleep at the table. The next morning, upon awakening, he discovered to his astonishment that the castle and all its occupants had disappeared and the land around him was desolate. The people on the road scorned and cursed him because he had brought the land to that condition by failing to ask questions. What he had not known was that the mysterious vessel that seemed to replenish itself had been the very thing he had been seeking, the Grail itself.

The ailing king might be likened to a discomforting situation; the Grail, that which can heal or rectify the condition. I do not here mean to oversimplify the symbolic content of so meaningful a tale, but only to attempt to show by its example the true nature and significance of a question, any question.

The question to be asked must be stated as simply as possible, and be answered by yes or no. Ideally, one should use the language of the *I Ching* in forming the question. This is somewhat difficult to do when first starting to use the book, for it necessitates more than a passing familiarity with the hexagrams and their meaning. Once one has begun using the book often, he should attempt to employ its language wherever possible. That is, once having understood the crossing of a great body of water as symbolic of a change of attitude (or whatever else one might decide the image to mean), when one has a question having to do with a change in attitude, he should ask if a crossing of the great water would be a favorable undertaking. Speaking to the book in its own language tends to heighten the "coincidence" of the answer. Therefore, there is not only the problem of correctly deciphering what the question in a situation should be, but also one of deciding how the question should be phrased.

There are times when one does not have a specific question in mind as, for instance, during those times when one is uneasy in spirit, unhappy without a cause, anxious for no reason, or simply empty of feeling or ideas. One may then simply throw a hexagram to discover the cause of his anxiety or uneasiness. The hexagram received at that time serves to localize the feeling, to nail it down so that one may set about resolving it.

To reiterate: The question should be as simple as possible, with phrasing as close to the language of the book as possible. Of course, this is not to say that the book will not supply an answer if these recommendations are not followed, but to point out that the answer received from this type of questioning will be as simple in its directness, as concise in its phrasing, and as meaningful as the question.

The Three Places

In the *Great Commentary* (*Ta Chuan*) we are told that the movements of the six lines of a hexagram reveal the way of three powers: the power of earth, the power of man, and the power of heaven. The first two lines of a hexagram are under the influence of the primal power of earth; the third and fourth, under the primal power of man; and the fifth and sixth, under the primal power of heaven.

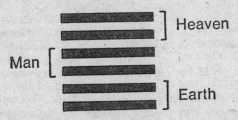

These three powers add another dimension to the hexagram, one which is in itself threefold. The hexagram, besides standing for a specific time or situation, also illustrates the cosmic unity of heaven, earth, and man, as well as diagramming the human body and the psyche. Although we will here look at these three aspects separately, it must be understood that in reality all three aspects are operative at one and the same time. It is only for purposes of analysis that they are presented separately here.

The three primal powers are three aspects of one spirit—the spirit Tao which, as the *Tao Te Ching* tells us, penetrates all things. When it penetrates the places of heaven, earth, and man it expresses itself as specific qualities.

I. *The Hexagram as a Diagrammatic of Cosmic Unity*

a. The Place of Earth
The activity of the spirit Tao as the primal power inherent

in earth becomes the active and regulating principle in biology and evolution, as well as in other cyclic phenomena. The place of earth, in this instance, is therefore dominated by the laws of nature. The cause of a situation outlined by either of the two lines occupying this place might be better understood if considered within this context: the course of action suggested, or the condition of the time, be it positive or negative, has come about because of the laws of nature. Another way to use this as an interpretative device is to understand that the way out of a predicament might be found within the context of such laws if not in direct application of them.

b. The Place of Man

Here, the activity of the spirit Tao as the primal power inherent in man becomes expressed as mores, values, tradition —in short, manmade laws.

c. The Place of Heaven

The place of heaven refers us to values that are eternal and spiritual. Here, the transformative process of the sequence, to be explained below, is operative.

II. *The Hexagram as the Human Body*

a. The Place of Earth

These two lower lines are always referred to in the *Book of Changes* as the lower limbs. Because the earth is regarded as feminine, warm, and moist, the place of earth in this instance is identified with the sphere of instinctual being, the place of passions and desires, or eros.

b. The Place of Man

This corresponds to the heart, the mediating principle between earth (eros) and heaven (logos). It mediates between the heat of the instincts and the iciness of the intellect.

c. The Place of Heaven

The head is the place of intellect and pure reason. Because the masculine principle in the *Book of Changes* is cold and dry, it represents the cold rationalism of intellect, the discriminating quality of mind that can sometimes be mercenary in its workings.

III. *The Hexagram as Model of the Psyche*

a. The Place of Earth

The Chinese believe that there are two souls active in the

body of man, one masculine, the other feminine. The feminine
or P'o soul has a downward-moving tendency and is always
busy attempting to drag down the active, outgoing male soul.
It seeks death. Its heaviness and sluggishness cause it to be
identified with earth. Its operations are those of sensuality
and anger. For this reason it may be identified with the Occidental concept of eros.

b. The Place of Man

This refers us to the ego, whose role is, ideally, to mediate
between, and cause the union of, the male and female souls.
If it cannot accomplish this before the death of the body, it
dissolves along with all personal characteristics, lost forever.

c. The Place of Heaven

Corresponding to the active, light, male principle, as the
female soul tends to move toward earth the active male principle tends toward heaven. If at death the ego has not united
the male and female souls, the male soul flies upward to reside for a time in heaven. It does not die. The female soul, on
the other hand, dissolves along with the body, becoming a
part of the element earth.

Before closing this section it should be mentiond that the
hexagram, all considerations of the three places aside, does
present us with a picture of the human body. The first line,
the toes; the second, the calves; the third, the hips; the
fourth, the trunk; the fifth, the jaws; the sixth, the head.

The Changed Hexagram

In First Principles we briefly mentioned the second or
changed hexagram resulting from changing or moving lines,
those having a numerical value of 6 or 9. Let us review.

If we throw Hexagram 48 with a 6 in the first place and a
9 in the fifth,

the resulting hexagram is Number 11, Peace, by virtue of the fact that 6's and 9's change into their opposites. The second or changed hexagram quite simply serves one of the three functions outlined below, or all three at once:

a. An amplification or modification of the first hexagram's statement;

b. A presentation of the inevitable outcome of the course of action outlined in the first hexagram, or the future result of the action having already taken place and pinpointed in that hexagram;

c. A prescription or remedy to either amplify or divert the results of the situation referred to in the first hexagram.

The problem of the changed hexagram and its proper interpretation is a thorny one and one that I believe is best left to each individual's conscience. At best, the three functions I present here are but a starting point. As always in hexagram interpretation, where words or logic fail us an intuitive, emotional, or suprapersonal "feeling" fills in the empty spaces. Let it guide you in this instance.

When one receives a hexagram with a changing line or lines, the textual and generalized comments on the nature of the hexagram should first be read, then the text accompanying the changing lines. The unchanging lines have little relevance to the answer received. Only when the unchanging line is specifically referred to in a changing line as having been the cause of the condition spoken of need it be consulted.

We find an example in line three of Hexagram 17, Following, where we are told that by clinging to the strong man one is guaranteed to lose the little boy. The little boy is the 6 in the second place, the strong man the 9 in the fourth place. If one had received this hexagram with only the 6 in the third place changing, it would be necessary for him to refer to lines two and four as well. By doing so, he would discover what qualities he must release himself from (those of a little boy) and what he should align himself with (those of a strong man). Not only would he discover what the proper course of action should be, but the very nature of the two qualities would then become clearly demarcated for him.

It is only fair to mention that in every hexagram there is a relationship of some significance between each line. To follow these relationships every time would be an excess; therefore, it is wiser to seek the nature of the relationship only when the text of the line itself makes comment on it, as in the example just given, or when following such a course appears absolutely essential in deciphering the answer to a question.

The next question that immediately comes to mind is, What does one do when changing lines are not received? As in the instance of changing lines, the generalized textual comments on the hexagram are to be read. Then, as a safety factor, one should read *all* the lines. A hexagram without changing lines indicates that one is standing before the time of the hexagram but has just come into the presence of the situation. One might say that the Tao of the hexagram has not yet become fully operative. It is as if one stood before a door preparing to enter. The lines of the hexagram must then be thought of as potentialities: When finally stepping through the door of the situation outlined by the hexagram, the individual may find himself *in* one or more of the lines. It is therefore wise to investigate the nature of the lines, for by so doing we discover the danger as well as the opportunities the time to come affords, thereby allowing us to enter the door in the proper way. In the appendix known as the *Great Commentary (Ta Chuan)*, we are told: "Peace is his who is conscious of danger; to him who looks lightly at things, the creation of his own downfall."

The Lines

The positions or places of a hexagram have yin and yang qualities assigned them. These positions must be understood as empty, the *quality* of their emptiness being yin or yang. An appendix of the *I Ching* tells us that the first, third, and fifth places are yang positions; the second, fourth, and sixth, yin.

In accordance with the philosophy of transformation and completion, a thing has successfully reached its end, its completion, when it resides in the place meant for it. This goes for man and objects as well as for the lines of a hexagram. For a yang line to occupy either the first, third, or fifth place is to have that line in the proper place. A yin line occupying any of those places is considered to be improper because the quality of softness occupies a place that demands firmness and perseverance. However, the "time" of the hexagram might indicate that the rigidity of the situation be diminished. Therefore, a yin line in a yang place may sometimes speak of a favorable event.

In Hexagram 28, Preponderance of the Great, we find one of several instances where a correct line in a correct place does not bring good fortune. The picture given us of the 9 in the third place, a yang line in a yin place, is of a beam sagging to the breaking point. The danger has come about because of the presence of excessive weight in a situation that is the personification of weight itself. Here, let us discuss the cause of the unfavorableness in what one would assume to be a favorable instance.

Simply put, it has to do with the nature of the hexagram itself. The hexagram speaks of a time of great preponderance, of great weight. The nature of the time is one of excessiveness. The recommendation is that one should have some place to go, that is, one should rid oneself of the prevailing attitude or situation that has brought about the time and arrive at a new one. One should not bring further weight to a time of excessiveness. The third place is a yielding, weak place. The heaviness of the yang line is the last straw. The time or situation of the hexagram either modifies or amplifies the nature of the lines and places, as it does the nature of the trigrams. This is an important point and one that will be referred to time and again throughout the book.

From the preceding it should be seen that the lines of a hexagram will often have significations assigned them that appear to have little connection with the attributes of either the hexagram or the trigram they are contained in. That is, because the quality of the place and the attribute of a line are modified by the time or situation of the hexagram in question, we may often find instances that appear to contradict all that has just been discussed.

In the simplicity of the hexagrams we find their complexity. In one instance we might find the general time of a hexagram modifying the qualities of line and place; at another, the lines and places modifying the condition exemplified by the total hexagram. This presents us with one of the most difficult problems in hexagram interpretation. Fortunately, it is not a vital point—the hexagram can still speak. Even so, it is important that one be aware of this particular aspect. We would therefore do well to discuss it a while longer.

To better show the many levels of meaning such modifications yield, let us consider the fact that the first line of a hexagram often presents the image of ground or sod—that which is firm and underfoot. In Hexagram 48, The Well, this particular aspect of the attribute is modified. The ground in this instance stands at the bottom of a well of water, and is now referred to as mud. The nature or the time of the hexagram has here not only modified the image often associated with the first line, solid earth, but by such modification or "watering" has made a weak yin line appear in a strong place, exemplified by the softness of mud.

Another image often associated with the first line is that of the foot or toes. All movement commences with the foot, but there are times when movement is not the action called for. In Hexagram 34, The Power of the Great, the first line is a yang line, or the force that is the very embodiment of action and movement, but the text of the hexagram tells us that it is in pausing that the Power of the Great shows itself. Obviously, the hexagram calls for a temporary cessation of movement; therefore the first line refers us to the idea that, because there is such power in the toes, to maintain such power in this instance would only lead one to misfortune. Here, a yang line in a strong place—one that would normally be considered proper—brings misfortune because the nature of the hexagram's time demands cessation of movement.

In another hexagram, Number 22, Grace, the yang line in the first place yields a favorable reading: One gives grace to one's toes because one leaves a carriage and walks. Here, the character of the line is affected by the character of the hexagram. This hexagram speaks of the necessity of attaining the grace and simplicity of unadorned form, tranquil beauty. To lend grace to one's toes is to leave the carriage and walk, for the Tao of toes *is* movement, and to be in Tao is to know grace. The nature of the yang principle is to move of its own accord, not to be carried about in a carriage. The fact that the first line is a yang line in its proper place indicates that the foot-image of the line is in proper relation with the time-image of the hexagram. In a time of grace, things should be as they inherently are, without adornment.

To reiterate: In both this hexagram and Number 34, the first line is a strong and active yang. In Number 34, a temporary cessation of movement is called for; therefore a strong line in a strong place is in this instance improper. In Hexagram 22, movement is called for; therefore the yang line in a yang place is proper, as it should be according to the rules the *Book of Changes* gives us.

We have just discussed the favorableness and unfavorableness of a yang line in a strong place. Let us now briefly look at a weak line in this first and strong place and close our discussion of the modifications created by both line values and hexagram condition.

In Hexagram 31, Influence, the idea of influencing others is portrayed by the image, where we are told that the superior man inspires and encourages people to move toward him. The hexagram calls for the power of influence, not movement—the people must come to the superior man, not vice versa. He is advised to remain still and cause things to move toward him. This idea is punctuated in each of the six lines. Starting from the first line, the toe, influence expresses itself in the calves of the legs, the thighs, mind, neck, jaws, cheek, and tongue. In every instance the attempt to influence in such a manner is unfavorable. The proper way to influence others is shown us by the picture the hexagram makes: a mountain with a lake in its hollow. In short, the superior man receives people by virtue of his emptiness, and he achieves this emptiness by keeping as still as a mountain, firm and resolute in his ways.

The yin and weak line in a strong place shows directed will. In this instance, because it is the beginning of movement it is not yet visible to the world, but the intent is there and that is where the danger and weakness lie. Here the weak line in a strong place is definitely unfavorable, for what is needed is the strength to abstain from movement; what is depicted here is a weak-willed person. A strong-willed person would not act in this way.

It should have become obvious to the reader at this point that the line of demarcation defining what is being modified by what—the hexagram by the lines, or the lines by the hexagram—is extremely thin. The guidelines are few, but in time one feels the correctness or incorrectness of the lines by merely seeing them.

In another hexagram containing a weak line in a strong place, also the first place, we are told that if one perseveres in keeping his toes still, no blame will be incurred. The hexagram is Number 52, Keeping Still. This hexagram calls for both physical and emotional restraint. By keeping the feet still, one makes no movement. A yin line, that speaking of quiescence, is in accord with the hexagram's general prescription: the stilling of the toes. On the other hand, the text also tells us that perseverance furthers. Because this is a weak line in a strong place, the keeping still might be thought of as the result of a certain weakness, the inadvertent result of a weak-willed person's actions, which in this instance work in his favor. The perseverance would therefore refer us to the necessity of consciously holding firm to the attitude arrived at by accident. This accidental good fortune is more than unlikely, however, because the book at all times addresses the reader as if he or she were the superior—but even the superior man must at times be subject to weakness.

The appendices to the *Book of Changes* go on to tell us that the first line of a hexagram is difficult to comprehend; the top line is easy. They also tell us that the first line speaks of the cause, the last line of the effect. Both the first and sixth lines are understood as standing outside the hexagram—the first referring to a man who has not yet entered the situation at hand, the second or sixth line to a sage who has not only left the situation behind him but the world as well.

To conclude: The second line is usually praised and is likened to an official at work in the country. He is praised because of the line's centrality, its being the center of the lower three-lined figure, or trigram; it therefore has a direct relationship with the ruler, the fifth line, which is also central and correct. The fourth line is the minister and is usually warned—the fourth line being so close to the ruler and, therefore, prone to think too much of itself. The third line is usually the object of misfortune. This comes about because of its weak position, standing at the transitional point between lower and upper trigram.

PART II

THE SEQUENCE

Before discussing the sequence of the *I Ching's* hexagrams, it will be necessary to make a distinction between the *visual* sequence and the *textual* Sequence. The visual sequence is that of the linear figures, the hexagrams, themselves; the textual Sequence is a text appended to the *Book of Changes*. Throughout this book, wherever the textual sequence is referred to the proper noun will be used; wherever the visual, a common noun.

The Visual Sequence

We know now that the sequence of the hexagrams in the *Lien Shan* and *Kuei Ts'ang* obviously differed considerably from the sequence we now find in the *Book of Changes*. The former opened with the hexagram for mountain, Hexagram 52, Keeping Still; the latter, with the hexagram for earth, Hexagram 2, the Receptive. We can also assume that the unusual but highly significant sequence of the book as we now have it, to be discussed below, was not then employed.

It will be noticed that the sequence composing the present-day book is made up of mirror images. That is, every odd-numbered hexagram is followed by an even-numbered hexagram whose line placement is of the same order, but inverted.

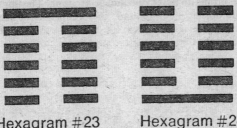

Hexagram #23   Hexagram #24

The exceptions are Hexagrams 1 (Heaven), 2 (Earth), 27 (The Corners of the Mouth), 28 (Preponderance of the Great), 29 (The Abysmal), 30 (The Clinging), 61 (Inner Truth), 62 (Preponderance of the Small). Visually, these hexagrams are opposite in structure owing to the fact that the mirror image of each of the above hexagrams result in the same image.

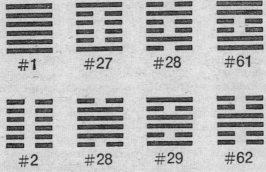

#1   #27   #28   #61

#2   #28   #29   #62

This sequence reiterates the theme presented us in the theory of the opposites, or yin and yang.

No other doctrine in Chinese history has affected its course as much as the doctrine of the opposites. Powers or forces responsible for all things in the world, the opposites came in time to be understood as the two expressions or aspects of one active and directing force, the Tao, or supreme ultimate. With the aid of the yin-and-yang doctrine the Oriental arrived at the position where he understood that there is an intimate relationship between things, between man and nature, and that reality is in a constant state of flux. The flux is a harmonious event, for the action of the opposites that brings it about is complementary and not conflictual. When yang, the active male principle, reaches its limit—that is, when activity reaches its end—yin, the tranquil, form-giving female is produced. When tranquillity reaches its end, activity again sets in.

The sequence we are discussing here is actually a metaphysical statement about the operation of yin and yang. It will be recalled that all odd numbers are male, all even numbers female. Because unity is expressed by the opposites in union, the complex of a yin and a yang, an odd-numbered hexagram and an even-numbered hexagram, can be thought of as constituting two aspects of one situation. When discussing the textual Sequence we will discover that the hexagrams actually refer us to situations. What the visual sequence reveals is that there are thirty-two such situations, each made up of an odd-numbered and an even-numbered hexagram. There are several ways this information may be employed.

One way has to do with viewing the complex of an odd-numbered hexagram followed by an even-numbered hexagram as the two sides of a coin or situation. The even-numbered hexagram, because of its maleness, represents the spirit in a situation. This is so because it is the male and active principle that initiates activity. In the Oriental's mind, the male initiates activity but is itself formless; substance, perceivable reality, comes into being only after the male principle has exhausted itself. The odd-numbered hexagram refers us to the outline of the situation as it exists in reality. If, therefore, we should receive Hexagram 62, Preponderance of the Small, in answer to a question, because it is an even-numbered and therefore feminine hexagram we could understand it to speak, as it does, of the handling of the smaller and seemingly insignificant aspects of a situation, rather than of the total situation or of any of its larger elements. The spirit of the situation, that which has activated it, would be revealed by the hexagram of which it is the mirror image—that preceding it. In this instance, that hexagram would be Number 61, Inner Truth. This is one example of how the sequence might be employed.

The second way of employing this information has to do with understanding the complex of an even-numbered and odd-numbered hexagram as representing the beginning and end of a situation. Because the male initiates activity, the odd-numbered hexagram might refer us to the beginning of the situation; the even-numbered, to the end of the situation.

As an example, Hexagram 41, Decrease, would speak of decreasing an aspect of the situation at its inception. At the situation's close, represented by the even-numbered hexagram, an increase of possibly that very same aspect decreased in the preceding hexagram would be called for.

In one instance the *I Ching* might, in answering a question, state that the received hexagram represents what is desired or correct rather than what is actually present in the situation. In this instance, the *I Ching* would be advising the inquirer to align himself with the precepts of the hexagram, because his present attitude is incorrect and must therefore be altered. On the other hand, the received hexagram might simply state *where one is* in relation to the situation. Hexagram 41, Decrease, might simply refer to the attitude one should assume. Here, the *I Ching* would not be telling one the "time" of the situation but rather that one should apply decrease to it. In this instance, the *I Ching* would be implying that the nature of the situation is already known to the individual, or that it is so apparent one need only look again to understand its nature. The hexagram received in answer to a question would be a prescription, a compound of different chemicals to be swallowed whole in order either to cure the symptoms of the situation or to maintain them.

Simply put, the visual sequence of the hexagram refers to the alternation of the opposites as the cause of the hexagrams changing into one another. It also presents the sixty-four hexagrams as a complex of thirty-two situations of bipolarity, on the one hand referring to the cause and nature—the spirit—of this situation, on the other to the result or form this spirit's activity causes to manifest itself in reality.

The Textual Sequence

In Book III of the Wilhelm translation we find a text called The Sequence, which in his translation is appended to each hexagram. In this Sequence we discover that every hexagram, or the time referred to by the hexagram, is viewed as the outcome of the preceding hexagram and the father of the hexagram that follows. As an example, the text of the Sequence appended to Hexagram 39, Obstruction, tells us that

the difficulties causing the obstruction have arisen because of
the opposition encountered in the hexagram preceding, Hexagram 38, Opposition. The hexagram following, Number 39,
Obstruction, tells us that because things cannot be permanently obstructed, the time of deliverance follows—Deliverance being the name of Hexagram 40.

In this Sequence, the Tao, or field of immediate knowledge, is here defined as a linear progression in time and
space. The archetypal situations, the hexagrams, are presented within a causal framework, indicating that a chance
occurrence, such as the reception of a hexagram, can only
occur against a static background. (The *I Ching* itself speaks
of change as that which does not change.) This progression
from one to sixty-four means that within any one field, or situation, there are sixty-four permutations that must be under-
gone before completion is achieved. That is, any and every
situation or idea has contained within it sixty-four phases that
follow one another in the sequence we find in the *I Ching*.
The hexagram one receives in answer to a specific question
tells one in which of the sixty-four stages the situation in
question is. By the same token, the total life situation, the
span from birth to death, might also be viewed as consisting
of sixty-four stages, as may the year, the month, the week,
the day, the hour. For this reason it is important that one
take notice of the hexagram preceding and the hexagram following the one received. The preceding hexagram informs
one out of what the present aspect of the situation has
grown; the following hexagram, what the next phase of its
development should entail.

That the Sequence states every situation or idea must go
through sixty-four transmutations before successfully achiev-
ing completion does not mean that every entry into a new situation finds one at the beginning of that situation. One might
enter a situation in its fiftieth phase, as represented by Hexagram 50, or in its third, Hexagram 3, Difficulty at the Beginning. Also, phases might be skipped, that is, one might progress from phase 30 to 64 in only one movement; in much
the same way one might be thought of as having slipped back
from phase 50 to phase 3.

But the most important statement the Sequence makes is
that there is a natural sequence in things. The darkness that
follows the light does so in accordance with a cosmic princi-

ple that states that anything developed to its fullest calls forth its opposite—that everything involves its own negation, that summer is followed by winter, life by death. One of the functions of the *I Ching* is to reveal to the individual a method by which he may align himself with the unending interplay of the opposites and thereby survive the tension generating from their coming together and separating. To be in Tao, therefore, one need but allow the interplay of the opposites to express themselves within the context of the Sequence, experiencing the tension as a flow rather than as a conflict.

Chinese cosmology states that the principle of activity, yang, precedes the principle of quiescence, yin. Once activity has achieved its fullest expression, quiescence manifests itself. The yin and yang forces represent the dynamic principles active in all things. Their first activity in the universe led to the creation of heaven and earth. Heaven, formless but active, is pure yang; earth, with form and substance, represents yin. As yang precedes yin, so heaven precedes earth in our sequence. The creator of the hexagram's visual sequence was expressing this metaphysical hypothesis when he placed Hexagram 1, Ch'ien, at the beginning of the book. Placing the hexagram of quiescence, K'un, immediately after it set the stage for the creation of the ten thousand things—a phrase used whenever all things in the world are referred to. It is obvious, therefore, that the ten thousand things are born as a result of the marriage of heaven and earth. That the creator or creators of the Sequence understood this to be the message of the visual sequence is borne out by the fact that no textual material having to do with the Sequence exists for the hexagrams of heaven and earth, Hexagrams 1 and 2. Heaven and earth are not part of the Sequence, they are the parents of the Sequence. All of the hexagrams in the *I Ching* trace the development of the product of the union of heaven and earth. As the Neo-Confucian, Chang Tsai, put it, "Nothing in the entire world does not understand heaven to be the father and earth to be the mother." Looked at from the cosmological point of view, the Sequence of the hexagrams outlines the stages of development growing out of the moment of genesis. The creation of the world and everything contained within it is here treated as the result of operations of mechanical principles in the universe. No deity or personified force stood be-

fore or above the process. The entire field of creation is understood as an operation of energy, the Tao, also referred to
as T'ai Chi, or the supreme ultimate. Again, Chang Tsai tells
us, "The process of production causes some things to come
first and others to come afterwards," and, "In producing
things, Heaven is known to have its sequence."

Because Chinese philosophers state that the supreme ultimate is the mind, we know that the operation that takes place
at the cosmic level in past, present, and future also occurs
within the field of human personality. The sequence of the
hexagrams therefore also outlines the developmental stages of
mind. From a larger perspective, the hexagrams speak of the
evolution of mind, its emergence, development, and completion. Therefore a number of the higher-numbered hexagrams
are prophetic in scope, for it is obvious that the evolution of
mind has not yet reached completion, obvious that we are
still in the beginnings. What hexagram represents the developmental stage the race is presently in is difficult to say. My
guess would be Hexagram 3, Difficulty at the Beginning. I feel
this because the marriage of heaven and earth is always at
first accompanied with a great deal of conflict. It is then
when the world of light, consciousness, rediscovers the world
of darkness, unconsciousness; when the perimeters (gates) of
the known world are opened to confront the dark unknown
surrounding it. But this is a personal view and of little use to
the reader. This short discussion of the implications to be
found by reading the *Book of Changes* as a revelatory book
outlining the inception, development, and goal of mind can
only point to the metaphysical problems this approach might
solve. Mere speculation to some, food to others.

Here a distinction must be made between the process and
the development of mind. The process of mind is a perma-
nent event; that is, the process cannot be halted or impeded
in any way. Neither can its development at the cosmic or evolutionary level be impeded. It is at the subjective level,
within the field of a personality, that development might be
halted. The process of mind is expressed by the interaction of
the five elements to be discussed in a later chapter. The developmental phases that this process attempts to activate is
represented by the sequence of the hexagrams.

For example: assuming that the development of consciousness within the personality is symbolically represented by the lineal progression of the sixty-four phases throughout an individual's life, one may easily see how one might "get stuck" in a phase for a lifetime. The activity, process, of mind would not halt, but its development would.

Conclusion

One thing apparent in both the visual and textual sequences is the idea that the sequence commences with the result of the union of heaven and earth. Hexagram 3, Difficulty at the Beginning, not only refers to the difficulty that besets union, but speaks of that which is born of union. The name of the hexagram, *Chun*, is defined as a sprout or blade of grass pushing itself up through the earth. The picture presented us by the hexagram is just that. The lower nuclear trigram is earth—therefore, a blade of grass beneath the earth. The upper trigram has as one of its significations difficulty; the upper nuclear trigram has as one of its significations that of a pressing down, a keeping still. The full picture, then, is of the earth pressing down on a blade of grass, thereby causing difficulty of birth.

Although neither the *I Ching* nor its commentators specifically refer to this idea, certainly the event depicted by this hexagram can be paralleled with the birth of new psychic material, idea, or awareness. The Oriental commentators who speak of the Tao as mind and of the trigrams as aspects of mind would have understood this to be the case. In any event, the Sequence as it now stands appears to bear out the thesis that the sequential arrangement of the hexagrams speaks of the development and transformations of mind itself at the evolutionary level, and of attitudes, ways of experiencing the world, at the individual level. A detailed display of this thesis and its ramifications is impossible in a book of this size. Therefore, a short and by no means comprehensive analysis of seven hexagrams in Sequence will have to suffice.

It should be obvious by now that the birth referred to in Hexagram 3, Difficulty at the Beginning, may be spoken of as allegorizing any number of "beginnings" or births. Because we are presenting the *I Ching* as an instrument of psychological or spiritual transformation, as a device outlining the pro-

cess of mind, we may here refer to the thing born as an attitude or a value.

Hexagram 48, The Well, tells us that although the organization of a town may undergo change, the well—here understood as standing at town's center—does not. The picture presented is that of the Ching T'ien, or "well-field" system of ancient Chinese social organization. A product of feudalism, the
system was one in which land that had been divided into a
large square was further subdivided into nine smaller squares.
Each of the outer eight squares was lived on and worked by
a family, the produce being theirs. The field of their lord, the
central and ninth field, was worked by all eight families, its
produce going to the overlord and his family. The well was
located in this central field. The word Ching, the Chinese
name for Hexagram 48, comes from this ancient arrangement. The ideogram here represents the nine fields.

Within the context of a transformative process, the hexagram is actually a statement about the psyche, or mind's organization. What we are referred to is the idea of a central
and unifying principle in the psyche that might be likened to
a well around which the components of the personality or, in
this instance, the components of an attitude—the townspeople and the town they compose—pivot. As the townspeople's
welfare is dependent on the availability and condition of the
well's contents, so too are the particulars of an attitude dependent on the psyche's central source of energy. The availability of this energy, or water, is of prime importance, making of the well's physical condition, as outlined by the hexagram, a matter of great concern. In discussing the well's condition and the state of its water, a system of introspection and
meditation is implied. Such willed and directed concentration
of consciousness is necessary to draw up the water from the
well.

In this instance, in Hexagram 48, we find the attitude, the
eight fields evenly distributed around the well, fixed. It is a
firm and orderly component of the individual's way of experiencing. He is content with his world view, for it allows him
to function with ease.

The Sequence appended to Hexagram 49, Revolution, tells
us that from time to time it is necessary that existing and stable structures be reorganized, revolutionized. This is in keep-

ing with the theory of the opposites: When something has achieved its end, change, of necessity, must occur—otherwise the structure becomes stagnant. The essence of change is creative reorganization. The implication here is that the operation of the individual psyche is based upon this fact. Here, the well is not changed, it is temporarily made inoperative while a cleaning operation commences. The very depths of the attitude are reconsidered, overhauled. As the events of the world are in constant flux, so too must the individual's value system be subject to constant revision in the face of new information and awareness.

Hexagram 50, the Ting, or Sacrificial Vessel, speaks not only of transformation but of the means of transformation: sacrifice. The old attitude must be willingly relinquished, consciously given over to the process of transformation. The established strictures of the old attitude are here given up so that a new formation, a newly organized well-field system, might emerge. This sacrifice of the old attitude must often be accomplished without knowing what the new attitude, the new anchor, might be. For that reason Hexagram 51, Shock and Thunder, follows this event.

The emergence of psychic energy, in this case in the form of a new attitude, is often a startling and terrifying event, for the new material has not yet been integrated into the conscious system. It is foreign and often causes confusion at first. The lightning and thunder of this hexagram speak of sudden enlightenment, awareness—the moment when we are confronted with the numen of the experience, the spirit before it is intellectualized into a parcel that consciousness can accept as meaningful.

Hexagram 52 is the time when contemplation of the event is called for. There, the individual is called upon to extricate himself from the excitement of the moment. He is to gain a stillness so that the event might come to a successful close. The success is that spoken of in the next hexagram in which we are told that things cannot stop forever, they must develop and move again.

The image of this hexagram is that of a young tree on a mountaintop, developing gradually. It is young, but hardier than the blade of grass of Hexagram 3 with which the process began. The prominence of the newly shaped attitude is indicated by the fact that there has been an ascension from the face of the earth, ground, to the mountaintop.

Throughout this sequence of Hexagrams 48–53 the emphasis has been on the workings of the opposites. In Number 48 movement has come to a complete close. In accordance with the law of the opposites, action in the form of revolution comes forth and reaches its peak in Hexagram 51, Thunder and Electrical Energy—the fullest expression of the yang as movement. Then the hexagram of keeping still emerges, only to be followed by the movement of development in Hexagram 53.

As in every aspect of hexagram interpretation, the information of the sequences is not always applicable. With practice and usage, the relevance of applying such information in certain instances will become apparent.

Chapter 3

THE EMBLEMS

Origin and Theory of the Five Elements (Wu Hsing)
or Five Stages of Change

The Four Ways

I

The greatest difficulty most people encounter in using the *I Ching* is the decipherment of the symbolic language it employs. If one simply reduces the symbols and images—that is, seeks out their original causes and actions—the difficulty is overcome.

In the line, "It furthers one to cross the great water," the basic idea is a transition from one place to another. Because of the book's age, we can be sure that at the time passing over a great water was a task that depended mainly on physical effort and stamina. Therefore, the line may be translated as meaning that it would be to the individual's advantage to expend a great deal of effort in the situation. But what is the purpose behind the expenditure of such effort? What does it mean to cross over a body of water? It simply refers to the idea of departing from one shore and arriving at another. Putting aside actual geographic relocation, where else does one find a departing and arriving in human life?

The dynamics of human personality often involve a revaluation and adjustment of position, often accompanied by a tremendous effort of will. This effort of will is that referred to as necessary to cross the great water; the crossing is actually the changeover from one attitude to another, or from one value to another. To cross the great water is to actually leave one's firm and comfortable position to arrive at another more fitting to the condition the individual finds himself in. On the other hand, one sometimes finds the recommendation not to cross the great water, meaning that a change of attitude is not favorable at this time, but that one should most definitely stick to the frame of mind or value presently held.

There is a danger here, as there often is in the interpretation of symbols, of assigning too literal an interpretation to the symbolic statement. One may easily mistake it as speaking of an actual, physical relocation in space. This danger may be easily circumvented if one bears in mind that all human action has its origin in instinctual and/or ideational responses. By listening to the suggestions of either his emotions or his common sense, one can be sure that one's physical responses to a situation have a greater possibility of being proper and correct. Because the contributors to the *I Ching* were acutely aware of this problem, they later appended to the book a system by which the individual might properly understand the metaphoric and symbolic meaning of the information contained in it. A piece of folk psychology, element theory—the moral and philosophical correspondences between man and the four elements—serves to insure against too literal an interpretation of symbols.

Since element theory was a spontaneous and independent product of many cultures throughout history, and since practically all such systems bear a marked resemblance to one another whether or not a transmigration of symbols transpired, we might say that they represent a structural and universal quality of mind. In contrast to other element theories, the system contained in the *I Ching* refers to the elements as ways of action rather than as types of personality. Throughout this work, I will ask the reader to bear in mind that such systems should be understood as only temporary supports. That is, the significations of the emblems and trigrams should be contained within you in such a manner that they may spontaneously rise to the surface of your mind as you view a hexagram. As a painter, poet, or musician prepares himself for the time when the creative spirit will manifest itself within him by attaining mastery of his tools, so too must you do with the emblems and trigrams, for each emblem and trigram is an archetype or symbol containing energy and information. But the objective is to let each symbol speak to your *own* condition. One could fill volumes on the symbolic significance of fire, but only those aspects that are significant to you are of any value. The *I Ching*'s objective is to help you construct or identify, strengthen and make tangible, the symbols you contain within yourself, those which as a rule manifest themselves only in dreams.

The Oriental, like everyone else, observed what was closest at hand and made it his yardstick. Observation of the heavens, the seasons, and the elements revealed to him the true nature of things. The most observable phenomena were the elements, the substances themselves—fire, earth, wood, water, and metal.

Origin and Theory of the Five Elements (Wu Hsing) or Five Stages of Change

In 213 B.C., during the Ch'in dynasty, a recommendation was placed before the emperor by the prime minister, Li Su. The recommendation had to do with the unification of thought in the empire and read as follows: "In the past, the world was confused and broken up . . . All that was of value to men was that which they had found in their private readings. Therefore, they caused to come into disrepute everything their superiors established. Now, your Majesty has brought the world together . . . Still we find those who . . . discredit the way of instruction and law . . . . If we do not stop this state of affairs, the imperial power will become weakened above and partisanships will undermine it from below." The prime minister then suggested that, to further unification of thought, all writings of the philosophers and

historians, and all other literature not having to do with agri-
culture, medicine, pharmacy, and divination, should immediately be handed over to the government for burning. This recommendation was approved and carried out. One of the
books that survived the holocaust was the *Book of Changes*.
Another, the *Shu King* or *Book of History*, disappeared. It
was not until the destruction of a summer house said to have
belonged to Confucius that a copy of that book was discovered in a wall. The *Book of History* contains information
pertinent to the *Book of Changes*.

The *Book of History* opens with an account of the great
deluge, supposed to have occurred around 2292 B.C. We must
remember that the Chinese firmly believed that the four seasons were regulated and controlled by the interplay of the
elements: earth, fire, wood, metal, and water. To insure pros-
perity and avert catastrophe it was the duty of the emperor
and his officials to properly perform the rituals traditionally
assigned each season. The inherent order of the cosmos had
to be faithfully duplicated here on earth. Failure to do so led
to catastrophe. The flood, we are told, came about because of
just such a failure. The superintendent of public works failed
to propitiate the element water during its season. Because of
this failure the element's positive features could not express
themselves.

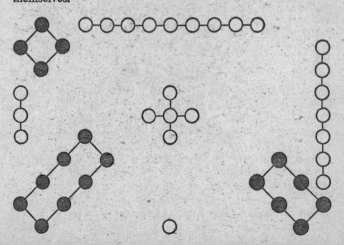

It was then the superintendent's responsibility to drain off the flood waters. After seven years of effort and continual failure, his job fell to the legendary hero Yu, who by partitioning the land into nine portions successfully drained it of its waters. As reward for his great labor and achievement, heaven conferred upon him The Great Plan and the Nine Classifications. These were recorded on the back of a great tortoise that had risen out of the Lo Shu. This diagram is known as the Writing from the River Lo.

According to tradition the source of this diagram is another known of as the Ho T'u, or the Yellow River map. The legendary hero Fu Hsi—in one place spoken of as having the body of a mountain, in another that of a serpent—discovered this map on the flank of a dragon-horse and supposedly based the construction of the *Book of Changes* on its information.

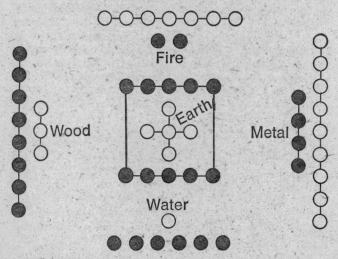

In both diagrams the dark circles represent yin, or earth; the light, yang or heaven.

In the tradition of Chinese popular thought it is believed that such a map existed almost from the beginning of time. Confucius himself reveals such a belief in the *Analects* (Book IX, Chapter VIII). Again, according to legend, the historical personage King Wen must obviously have had access to such a diagram in order to construct the diagram known as The Sequence of Later Heaven. It is now known that neither King Wen nor his son the Duke of Chou had anything to do with the construction of the *Book of Changes,* much less with either of the three above-mentioned diagrams.

It is the Great Plan (Hung Fan) chapter of the *Book of History* that speaks of the elements and their nature. To paraphrase, the element water is that which soaks and descends; fire, that which blazes and rises up; wood allows curves and straight lines to be made on it, thereby accepting form from cutting instruments; metal is moldable in the liquid state, and then becomes firm and solid; earth produces edible vegetation. Because the symbolic correlations of the elements are so much a part of early Chinese thought, it must be assumed that the Confucian creators of the appendices accompanying the *Book of Changes* not only knew of them, but in assigning the emblems and the trigrams to the cardinal points of the compass also sought, whether consciously or unconsciously, to add yet another significant layer of correlation on the elements traditionally occupying those points. When contemplating the emblems and trigrams, one should keep these correlations in mind, for they sometimes yield information of inestimable value in hexagram interpretation.

For this reason, I list here the traditional Chinese symbolic correlations of the elements.

The element wood is located in the east. The season it rules is spring, and it expresses itself in wind. It is the essence of the stars, and its planet is Jupiter. Its heavenly animals are the tiger and the hare; its earthly animal, sheep. All scaly animals, such as fish and serpents, are under its dominion. In the human body, its nature is found in the muscles, works through the spleen, and has to do with the operation of the eye. Its expression is that of anger. Its taste is sour, its odor that of a goat. It is green in color, and its number is 8.

The element fire is located in the south. The season it rules is summer, and it expresses itself in heat. It is the essence of the sun, and its planet is Mars. Its heavenly animals are the horse and serpent; its earthly animal, fowl. All feathered animals are under its domination. In the human body, its nature is found in the pulse of blood, works through the lungs, and has to do with the operation of the tongue. Its expression is that of joy. Its taste is bitter, its odor that of burning. It is red in color, and its number is 7.

The element earth is located in the center. It has no season assigned it, but does express itself in thunder. It is the essence of the planet Earth and its planet is Saturn. Its heavenly animals are the dog and ox; its earthly animal, the ox. All naked (hairless) animals are under its dominion. In the human body, its nature is found in the flesh, works through the heart, and has to do with the operation of the mouth. Its expression is that of desire. Its taste is sweet, its odor fragrant. It is yellow in color, and its number is 5.

The element metal is located in the west. The season it rules is autumn, and it expresses itself in coldness. It is the essence of the constellations, and its planet is Venus. Its heavenly animals are the cock and the monkey; its earthly animal, the dog. All hairy animals are under its dominion. In the human body, its nature is found in the skin and hair, works through the kidneys, and has to do with the operation of the nose. Its expression is that of sorrow. Its taste is acrid, its odor rank. It is white in color, and its number is 9.

The element water is located in the north. The season it rules is winter, and it expresses itself in rain. It is the essence of the moon and its planet is Mercury. Its heavenly animals are the bear and the rat; its earthly animal, the pig. All animals with shells are under its dominion. In the human body, its nature is found in the bone marrow, works through the liver, and has to do with the operation of the ear. Its expression is that of fear. Its taste is salty, its odor that of something rotten. It is black in color, and its number is 6.

The ideas appearing in the Great Plan section of the *Book of History*, those dealing with element theory, are now taken to be if not the creation of Tsou Yen, at least the result of his synthesization and the stabilization of theories held by a great number of Chinese thinkers. His dates are uncertain, but can be located somewhere between the beginning of the fourth and middle of the third century B.C. Tsou Yen is recognized as being the father of alchemy in China. This is of some relevance, for, as we shall see in the chapter on the trigrams, later Taoist and Neo-Confucian philosophers treated the *Book of Changes* and its diagrams as alchemical devices.

The Four Ways

II

The emblems are the four two-lined figures resulting from the combination of yin and yang lines. They represent four of the five Wu Hsing, or elements, and are recognized by the following yin and yang combinations:

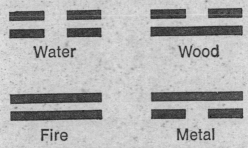

Water Wood

Fire Metal

The fifth element, earth, does not have an emblem assigned it because, as the element the other four sprang out of and return to, it is potentially present in each of them.

Let us see how the emblems are contained in Hexagram 39, Obstruction.

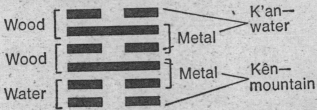

The first and second lines compose the emblem water; the second and third, metal; the third and fourth, wood; the fourth and fifth, metal; the fifth and sixth, wood. As you can see, only three of the four emblems are present in this hexagram. The text for this hexagram reads, "Water on the mountain: the image of Obstruction." As we shall see in further detail when we discuss the trigrams, the fourth, fifth, and sixth lines compose the trigram K'an, water; the first, second,

and third, the trigram Kên, mountain; therefore, the six together read water on the mountain. As a rule the text, called
the image, accompanying every hexagram refers to the picture made by the two trigrams. These images are the simplest
the creators of the book could devise, and simple they had to
be if they were to be accessible to a general public. But there
are many other images present that sometimes better reveal
the reason behind the hexagram's name. We have such an instance in this hexagram.

For clarity's sake, let us set the first and second lines aside
and look just at the third, fourth, fifth, and sixth lines:

Notice that the fourth and fifth lines compose the emblem
metal and that the two emblems above and below it—the
third and fourth, fifth and sixth lines—represent wood. The
picture is of a piece of wood cut in half by a piece of metal.
The growth of wood has been obstructed by this cutting action. In this instance, the emblems yield a better picture of
the condition referred to by the hexagram than the trigrams
composing it. So far we have a clearer picture, but no further
elucidation.

Throughout the *I Ching* several allusions are made to the
effect that the four emblems definitely are interpretative devices. The commentary on the decision accompanying Hexagram 42, Increase, frankly states: "The way of wood creates
success."

Let us now approach the elements the way the ancients
did, noting their properties and effects in nature first, and
then applying the information to the human condition.

The Way of Water

The Way of water is manifold. Water assumes the shape of
whatever container it is placed in, the same way an idea
eventually assumes the shape of the containing attitude or situation it first manifests itself in.

Itself shapeless, water gives form to things by nourishing

them. It is the nourisher of all things, feeding and sustaining both plant and animal life. From this one might say that the Way of water is expressed any time an idea or situation is "fed"—maintained and kept alive.

The movement of water is downward. To nourish things water moves from the surface of the earth to its interior. This could be taken to be expressive of a contemplative method. Because water is formless and moves in this manner, another Way of Water is letting things happen within the scope of a contemplative attitude, not attempting to delineate or give form to the situation at hand, letting the situation and its particulars find their own way unhampered. This might be the analysis of a favorable line within a hexagram—a line, that is, contained within the emblem for water. In Hexagram 56, line one, we find: "If the wanderer busies himself with trivial things, he draws down misfortune upon himself." This situation might have come about because no form was present, because in this instance the formlessness of water should have been given form, a vessel or path by which it might reach the thing it was to nourish.

The Way of Fire

The Way of fire is concerted effort, heated or fevered application. In imitating fire, one should start slowly, and then rapidly encompass the situation at hand. Where the emblem fire contains an unfavorable line, one may assume the situation has come about because of impatience or an unthinking headlong rush into the heart of it. In a favorable line, the suggestion would be to act in just such a manner, to approach the matter without further thought.

The Way of fire also signifies clarity and intellectual effort, for it is by the light of fire that things are seen. Therefore an unfavorable line might speak of an absence of such clarity, of the individual's failure to carefully shed light on and inspect the problem in question. A favorable line, on the other hand, might mean that he has done or should do just that.

Because fire moves upward it is expressive of an open and outward-looking attitude. When a line is unfavorable, one may say that the situation has come about because one has not responded in this manner.

Fire transforms things, but a successful transformation by fire depends on proper application and control. In all we have said about fire, this is the key factor. Too much fire destroys while it transforms; too little achieves nothing.

The Way of Wood

The Way of wood is defined by the action of living wood. While fire has an upward movement dependent on that which it encompasses, on that which it devours and transforms, the upward movement of wood has the added quality of expansion. The Way of wood is a much slower process. It takes time for wood to grow. Also, wood not only moves upward, it moves downward, imperceptibly.

The movement of wood is threefold: upward into the realm of light, where it expresses itself in full foliage; downward into the realm of darkness, where it receives the greater part of its nourishment; and outspreading. The latter movement is expressed in two ways: the outspreading of the branches, which shade and conceal the event itself—a movement expressive of the gentle and protective care given an idea or situation; and the invisible, but nonetheless significant, outspreading of the roots. All of these movements are imperceptible and slow. There is nothing hurried here. The roots of a tree have a firm foothold in the earth upon which it is dependent for its nourishment and may therefore be likened to the genetic, racial, spiritual, or religious roots of the individual. The earth they grasp is the body of the tradition he sprang from—that aspect of personality upon which one relies, has faith in.

The way of action expressed by the emblem for wood is a slow and persevering one. It speaks of an expansion of attitude, an all-embracing approach or openness, which, though free in expression, is firmly rooted in substance and capable of discrimination. The *Book of History* tells us that the Way of wood is crooked, which brings to mind Shakespeare's statement that one sometimes must "through misdirection find direction out."

The Way of Metal

In fire, wood, and water we find movement as an inherent principle. Metal is static, inactive. Metal does not *do* anything. It has things done to it. It is solid and without movement. For it to be of any use, it must be formed and shaped.

True, metal can cut and penetrate things, but not of its own accord—it must be wielded to achieve such ends.

The Way of metal, therefore, is the way of not doing, but of letting "have done to."

On the other hand, the Way of metal might also be understood as one of firmness. Let things be done to you, but stand as firm as metal, yielding only at the point where the tension of the situation may bend or crack you. Then, as metal, allow yourself to be reshaped. As a rule, the emblem suggests that one should be as hard as metal, as uninvolved as metal. In an unfavorable line, the unfavorableness of the situation might have come about because of just this type of action, a stance of unemotional involvement.

III

With this material at hand, the *I Ching*'s statement that one should rely on "the emblematic figures for definite action as in the construction of implements" should now be relevant. The emblems stand for the concretization of the attitude arrived at through viewing the changes. In other words, the way the changes of a hexagram are to be made real in the world is determined by the way of action depicted by the emblems the changes are contained in.

As a general rule, the application of these interpretative aspects of the emblems should only be employed when one is confronted with a line in movement, a changing line. This is the time when such information is particularly pertinent. This is not to say that these significations should be employed only at that time, but that the efficacy of the significations become much more apparent with moving lines than with unmoving lines.

Before closing this section, let us apply the foregoing information to a hexagram—Hexagram 22, Grace.

The first two lines of this hexagram comprise the emblem for wood. Here, the imperceptible growth of wood, its deliberateness, is symbolized by the labor of walking. During the time of grace—adornment, as the hexagram's ideogram is literally translated—a slow and humble progress rather than quick and luxurious transportation as in a carriage, is not only correct but rewarded. The first line of the emblem, counting from the bottom up, is a strong line in a strong place. During a time of grace, of refinement, the proper course of action is to employ the natural strength and energy of the line and place, to lend grace to one's toe by leaving the carriage.

At the top of the line of the wood emblem, the movement initiated by the first line is warned. The labored but graceful movement can easily lead to nothing more than a gesture, an imitation of grace. To devote time to furthering such a gesture, to work on outward appearance for its own sake, is little more than vanity. Once one leaves the carriage he might think himself too grand, or might find that he has left the carriage for no other reason than to appear as such. As a beard is but an adornment, so too can what was once a noble gesture become but an adornment. How may one guard against this? By following the way of metal, of which this is the first line.

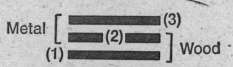

When one works a piece of metal the aesthetic value of its form is dependent on the piece's content. Here, one should let oneself be the thing formed instead of the thing forming; one should not form gestures and attitudes for the beauty or effectiveness of their form, but should let the inner experience, the value arrived at through the gradual development exemplified by wood, form the outward appearance.

The top line of the metal emblem is line three. Having achieved the conditions of this line, having passed the danger spoken of in the second line, one may become too proud of one's achievement, rest on one's laurels, become intoxicated by one's hard-won success. So, one is told to remain as constant and persevering as metal—immovable in purpose and intent, cold and indifferent to the enticements of success.

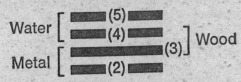

The fourth line is the top line of the wood emblem. The first line of this emblem was the third line and, in conjunction with the attributes of metal, spoke of the perseverance of wood; here we see the line as the first of the water emblem. The tendency of water to flow downward, that is, inwardly, is alluded to. The doubt surrounding this line is dissolved by such contemplation.

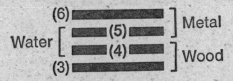

At the top line of the water emblem and the first line of the metal emblem, the fifth line, the turning away from the exterior world through a contemplative act, leads one to experience shame. His material gifts and belongings are few. Despite the humiliation one should be persevering as water in his simplicity and find his strength in the example of metal.

The top line, the sixth, is the top line of the metal emblem. Here the recommendations of line three have been successfully followed. All ornamentation has been washed away. Content has shaped form.

Chapter 4
THE TRIGRAMS
PART I

The Sequence of Earlier Heaven: The Primal Arrangement

Of all elements in the *Book of Changes* the eight three-lined figures known as trigrams are unquestionably the most significant. Without an understanding of these figures, much of the book's message is lost. In discussing them it will be necessary to start at the beginning, but because so much of the beginning has been lost in history we will be forced to construct the logic of the book's originators from the ideas existing at that time. In doing so we hope to answer two major questions: "Why are there only eight trigrams?" and "Why are there only sixty-four hexagrams?"

We have discussed in an earlier chapter the fact that the theory of the opposites is an indigenous product of Chinese thought, and that the pictorial representation of these opposites, yin and yang, grew out of the tortoise-shell divination to yield the notation system of a broken and unbroken line:

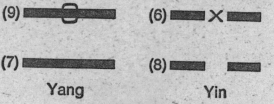

Yang   Yin

It is to be also remembered that the theory of the opposites states that each opposite contains its own negation, or its opposite. That is, if an opposite were to be dissected it would be found to be made up of two parts, a positive and a negative pulse. The yang or masculine opposite would therefore look, in such a schematic diagram, like this:

and the yin like this:

That division leads to duality is an accepted fact in Chinese thought. The original and supreme force, the supreme ultimate or T'ai Chi, upon division yielded the opposites. There would be no reason, therefore, why this division should not become the active and dynamic nature of the universe, as well as its cause and continuing process.

The first three divisions would therefore look like this:

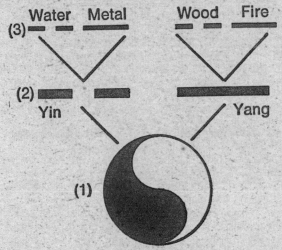

The Supreme Ultimate

In his *Observation of Things*, Shao Yung tells us: "After the Supreme Ultimate divided, the Two Forms were revealed." The two forms he refers to here are the yin and the yang. Again, he says: "The Supreme Ultimate is a unity. It does not move. It gives birth to a duality which is Spirit. Spirit yields number, number yields emblems, and the emblems yield objects."

It will be noticed that the two tiers presented here yield the four emblems discussed in the last chapter. Viewing the diagram from the bottom up we discover the genealogical statement: The supreme ultimate is father and mother of the opposites. The duality of the original unity is here separated into two distinct qualities. The first step in its differentiation has been achieved and yields the first distinction: male and female, dark and light, etc. These two principles then continue the work of the original division by becoming parents themselves. The yang gives birth to the two emblems of fire and wood; the yin gives birth to water and metal. This is the second differentiation. At the same time, according to Shao Yung, the first differentiation yields spirit. That is to say, yin and yang are the two aspects of one spirit, one energy. The one could not exist without the other. The hermaphroditic nature of spirit is a theme that occurs again and again in all discussions of spirit throughout the centuries. It is, therefore, not unusual to find it here as well. Because the original unity is a "oneness" that has not yet reflected on its own nature, its division is momentous. It suddenly realized duality, the first expression of number. The language of spirit, it appears, is number. The great Christian mystic, Nicholas of Cusa (1401–1464), said: "Number is the first model of things in the mind of the Creator." His statement grows out of the Platonic and Pythagorean traditions of Western culture, which in time synthesized to become the numerological statements of Christianity, the most familiar being the concept of godhead as trinity. Plato was alive sometime during the period 428–347 B.C., at about the same time the numerological concepts of the Chinese were being independently developed. This coincidence in time indicates that we are in the presence of an archetypal statement, a universal: Spirit first expresses itself as number, the first number being two, that of the opposites. In the Chinese system number yields the four emblems, or elements. The original spirit undergoes a further refinement: It becomes the four essences, which will in time become the spirit in matter, for the four emblems do not represent the elements themselves but their essences. They are insubstantial, subtle bodies without form.

Finally, the emblems yield objects. That is to say, they yield the representations of substance. This is diagrammed as follows:

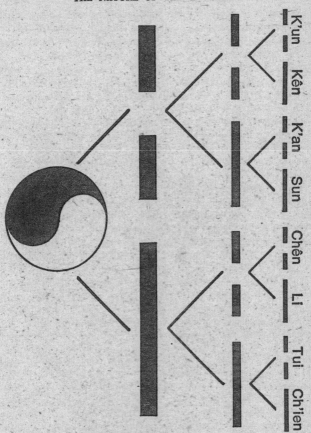

K'un

Kên

K'an

Sun

Chên

Li

Tui

Ch'ien

We are now in the presence of the eight trigrams, four of which, reading the diagram from the bottom up, have as their essence the yin principle, and four of which have as their essence the yang principle. But we have not yet answered the first question, "Why only eight trigrams of three lines, instead of sixteen trigrams of four lines each, as a fourth tier in the diagram would yield?"

In the chapter discussing the hexagrams we spoke of the three places of a hexagram: the place of man, earth, and

heaven. These three distinctions were dominant in the mind
of the Oriental from the beginning. The *Book of Odes,* a
product of the eighth century B.C., notes throughout that the
Chinese constantly thought in terms of this triplicity. In time
they began to speak of three powers, the three manifestations
of spirit in heaven, in earth and in man. The creators of the
Book of Changes would have had these distinctions in mind
when creating a book that purported to explain the workings
of these three realms in unity, and would have explained the
workings of the opposites within that context. Their solution
was a simple one: Taking the yin and yang as the active principles in the universe, man, and earth, let us show the fullest
field of their action. Taking a figure of three lines as representative of the three major distinctions of heaven, earth and
man, and combining the two principles in all possible combinations, the yield is a complex of eight three-lined figures. All
possible combinations of yin and yang within a mold of three
lines yields neither more nor less. But, as the *Book of
Changes* tells us, the appearance of these eight trigrams only
signals what is called a "small completion." Shao Yung adds
that the first two tiers, those making up the emblems, that by
which heaven might be identified, is produced; with
the third tier, those making up the trigrams, that by which
earth might be identified is produced. The important point
here is that we are in the presence of the archetypal ideas of
what is yet to come. The stage has been set. The archetypes
after which everything is to be modeled have been given
form. It is a small completion. In the diagram of the three
tiers we are presented with a model of the archetypal realm
of which all things are mere reflections. In the appendix of
the *I Ching* known as the *Great Commentary,* we are told:
"In the Changes there is the Primal Beginning (supreme ultimate). This yields the two forces (yin/yang). These in turn
yield the four emblems, and the four emblems yield the eight
trigrams."

In a later chapter discussing the lines, this idea is amplified
to make the final statement: "The Tao of heaven, earth, and
man are contained in the *Book of Changes.* It takes these
three primal powers and doubles them. This is the reason
why there are six lines. The six lines are but the ways of the
three powers." The doubling, or further division of this
three-tiered diagram, yields what is known as the diagram of
the supreme ultimate:

Here we have all sixty-four of the hexagrams. The reason why the eight trigrams are doubled has to do, again, with the principle of duality in the universe. During the time of this doubling that which existed in archetypal form now takes on substance. The sixty-four hexagrams represent the field of activity known as the world. Tracing back to origins—that is, from the top of the diagram of the supreme ultimate to the first tier—we discover the parent of the situation depicted by the hexagram. This doubling constituted the great and final completion.

The diagram of the supreme ultimate is a valuable tool in hexagram interpretation. Its implications are far-reaching and can only be touched upon here. Consider: If one received Hexagram 62, Preponderance of the Small, and found its place on the diagram (the thirteenth hexagram from the left), by tracing the connecting line down to the third tier he would discover that the archetype that gave birth to this hexagram is Kên, the mountain, and that the principle that is parent to it is yin. Looking at the place in the fifth tier where this hexagram is connected, he would then discover that the fourteenth hexagram from the left shares its origins. This other hexagram is Number 56. The Wanderer. In Preponderance of the Small we are told success will come to us by doing small things; in The Wanderer the same message is given us: success through smallness.

Counting from the left again, we find that the ninth and tenth hexagrams, Numbers 15 and 52, respectively, spring out of the same place in the fifth tier. Hexagram 52, Keeping Still, advises one to reduce movement. In Hexagram 15, Modesty, one is told to pause in this movement to find balance.

Work with this diagram. The "coincidences" yield considerable information. Let us now return to the trigrams.

The Sequence of Earlier Heaven: The Primal Arrangement

It will be discovered that if one takes the first three tiers of the diagram of the supreme ultimate, causing the first four trigrams (counting from the left) to ascend along the right portion of a circle, the final four up the left side, we arrive at the following diagram:

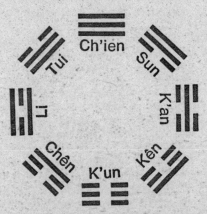

This diagram, appended to the *Book of Changes* through-out the centuries, is known as the sequence of earlier heaven, or primal arrangement. In it we are presented with the tri-grams as pairs of opposites. Heaven and earth are at opposite poles, as are fire and water. This diagram is the nucleus of the *Book of Changes*. Anyone who can fully comprehend the workings of this diagram need never own a copy of the book. It is unlikely that such a person exists, for this diagram is in essence the universe itself. The source of this diagram is be-lieved to be the Lo Shu, or Writing from the River Lo, briefly mentioned in the chapter on the emblems.

For draining the floodwaters that had inundated China, Yu was presented the Great Plan, wherein the nine classifications and the five elements were recorded. After assigning a nu-meral to each of the nine classifications he recorded the plan on the back of the great tortoise. The image of the great tor-toise was of considerable significance to the ancient Chinese, for to them it spoke of tortoise-shell divination. As explained earlier, tortoise-shell divination involved the application of a heated metal rod to the belly of a tortoise. The crack or con-figurations that then occurred revealed aspects of the future.

The significance of this tale lies in the idea that the appli-cation of heat to a belly results in knowledge of past, present, and future. If myths are truly the result of archetypal infor-mation projected into the world, we should be able to find a parallel instance of this idea in actual application. And we do have such an instance in the Hindu practice of Tapas, or interior heat.

In practically every yogic system of the Near or Far East the attempt to fuse the polarities expressive of the human condition, the attempt to reintegrate the personality and return it to the unity at the base of all creation, fire appears as the element needed to achieve that end. That fire is taken to be an interior or spiritual fire, Tapas, which is located in either the belly or the heart, each organ often acting as a synonym for the other. We know from mythology that the belly or womb is recognized as being the place of transformation. In the womb life appears to manifest itself out of nothing; in the belly, matter is transformed into energy. It is not unusual, then, to find the ancients regarding these two areas as being similar in purpose and construction to the universe, where all wisdom abounds.

Simply speaking, the practice of Tapas speaks of an intensification of consciousness by a willed directing of all psychic or emotional energies inward, toward an imagined or real center—toward that region we have defined as the objective psyche. With the aid of this highly developed method of introversion the individual comes to know and learn things beyond the limits of average consciousness, for, as the *Rig Veda* tells us, "Out of the flaming Tapas order and truth were born."

In tortoise-shell divination we find an intimation of this process. In yoga the act becomes internalized, the projection withdrawn from the world. Tortoise-shell divination is a physical expression of the mechanics of intuition, intuition in its most primitive form. In yoga, in this instance, we find a despiritualization of the world, a withdrawal of a projection, performed in the proper way. The world is despiritualized so that the interior man may become spiritualized. With the rise of rationalism in the Occident in the seventeenth century, a similiar despiritualization occurred in the name of science, but the projected value of information was discarded. Western man did not then understand that the universe was an integrated whole dependent on each of its parts. The spiritual and social eruptions we now witness are the result of our failure to recognize this truth.

The tortoise in our tale, therefore, is the carrier of wisdom. He not only knows the secret depths of the primal ocean, the objective psyche, but carries the secret in his belly. His ability to live in the element water and on the element earth symbolically identifies him as being a mediator of contraries. Wisdom and intuition unite the opposites.

In passing, let me add that the intensification of consciousness, the heat of introspection, is symbolized in our little tale by the heated metal rod that is applied to the tortoise's belly.

What is the diagram Yu draws on the back of the tortoise? The diagram of earlier heaven is a cosmic diagram in that it is a visual representation of cosmogonic ideas. It outlines concepts of time and eternity, delineates the boundaries of the earth, and reveals the manner by which the cosmos interacts with the mundane sphere of existence. It is a magic circle or mandala.

A mandala is essentially a visual representation of the cosmos, its function in the Orient being to aid the devotee in his endeavors to become reintegrated with the divine order of cosmic reality. In the simplest mandala we find the four cardinal compass points represented as either deities or powers. But the most important point in all such diagrams is the center where the totality of the powers in each cardinal point resides, either as a god or a metaphysical concept—the point, that is, from which the universe is generated.

The mandala's first function is the delineation of both temporal and cosmic time and space. It is an essential function, for to be oriented in time and space is to be cognizant of being, to have a consciousness of self. I speak here not of the consciousness we normally identify with sensory awareness, but rather of that consciousness which knows itself as one contained within a continuum, historical or personal.

The devotee's objective is to identify himself with the power residing at the center. The mandala is imagined or realized as contained within the devotee himself, his body thereby immediately gaining the proportion of a macrocosm. Once again, intense concentration is the keynote. By successfully identifying himself with the center, the devotee unites the microcosm with the macrocosm, making of the two one. The conflict and tension existing between these two dimensions are dissolved and the personality is reintegrated with the unity of the cosmos. It is through the method of Tapas outlined above that this is achieved.

C. G. Jung noticed that during certain stages in the analysis of the unconscious when moments of either extreme crisis or conflict occurred, the majority of his patients drew or painted mandalas. His conclusion was that in any deep and lasting penetration of the unconscious, in any attempt to unite the opposites, the individual suffers a disorientation, a decentering, and that the appearance of the mandala is the psyche's announcement that an attempt has been made to recenter and rearrange the components that make it up. The visual representation of this psychological process is the mandala. The mandala, therefore, in Oriental usage, and hopefully in future Occidental usage, serves as a portal of safe entry and return into the deeper layers of our being, into the realm of the objective psyche, home of the spirit. Such is the nature of the diagram drawn on the back of the great tortoise. It is a mandala which we must take into ourselves so that the hexagrams might manifest their message in and through us.

In tortoise-shell divination a physical manipulation of objects was involved, the manner and method known to few. It was not open to every man. Wisdom was reserved, hidden in the underbelly of the tortoise. The secret of the *I Ching* is permanently sketched on the back of the tortoise, in full view and accessible to all men. What we have in the myth is the historical moment when the transition from tortoise-shell divination to yarrow-stalk divination occurred, when macrocosm and microcosm were brought closer to one another by a further differentiation of consciousness. Through this diagram, and with the aid of the book that has been made manifest by it, man may learn to speak with cosmos.

The trigrams situated at the eight compass points are formed of yin and yang, the original expression of the objective psyche's or spirit's division. The spirit Tao manifests itself in the world as two distinct entities that complement each other: Yin is dark, yang is light. The *I Ching* also tells us that the activity of the various elements in this diagram is that of pure spirit.

Wang Chung (A.D. 27–97) writes: "Some maintain that man carries the fluid of Heaven and Earth in his bosom. This fluid in the body is mind . . . the thoughts are one's own spirit . . . What we see while awake, or hear while asleep, is all the work of our Spirit." That the fluid of heaven and earth, or yin and yang, becomes mind in the body, is to reiterate the point made earlier: The spirit has a suprapersonal origin and source common to all men. In Chinese philosophy that source is the great primal beginning, or supreme ultimate.

About this great primal beginning, Shao Yung says, "The mind is the great Ultimate." This supreme ultimate is the basis of all mind, it is the primal pool of energy or objective psyche. The Chinese tell us that in the beginning this pool was in a great state of chaos, undifferentiated. At some point it separated out to give birth to heaven and earth, or yin and yang. The *Huai-nan Tzu* says: "Tao covers heaven and earth . . . There is no limit to its height, and its depth is unfathomable." Once heaven and earth came into existence, became distinct qualities, Tao itself became definable. If the supreme ultimate is mind, and in its act of splitting yields the opposites, yin and yang, our next question is: "What in the human psyche might be likened to yin and yang?"

To possibly answer this question it will be necessary to decipher the following statement: "Heaven, earth, infinite space, and infinite time are the body of one person, and the space within the six cardinal points is the form of one man. Therefore he who understands his nature will not be threatened by heaven and earth."

The six cardinal points referred to in this quote are six of the eight trigrams diagrammed in the primal arrangement. The other two are those of heaven and earth. The statement brings out the idea that the interplay of heaven and earth, the opposites, is not only threatening but dangerous. In order to escape the threat of the opposites one must become so familiar with their operations that he can anticipate their every action, thereby preparing himself for the event. To learn the nature of their natural operation is to diminish the tension of their interplay—that which manifests itself in the psyche as a threat, an anxiety and uneasiness of being. That all of infinite space and infinite time are contained within one is to say that the ground of human personality is the objective psyche. The Oriental here says that the structure of the psyche is that outlined in the diagram of the primal sequence.

In the *Book of Changes* yin and yang are represented by heaven and earth, Ch'ien and K'un. That the diagram of the primal arrangement was considered mandalic and understood as residing within the individual is borne out by the miscellaneous notes appended to Hexagram 37, The Family. There we are told that the family is inside. This refers to the fact that the trigrams are understood as a family unit of mother, father, three daughters, and three sons. Furthermore, the Commentary on the Decision appended to this hexagram states that the place of the woman is within and that the place of the man is without—that is, the receptive and devoted quality of yin should be experienced inwardly, whereas the active and creative movement of being must be expressed outwardly. It goes on to tell us that in order for a house to be set in order the father should be as a father, mother as a mother, and children as children. Only in that way does the world become orderly. In other words, the components of personality symbolized by the trigrams must be placed in their proper relationship to one another if one is not to be threatened by heaven and earth. Here we find the Confucian rectification of names employed as a psychological device.

Holding the above in mind and recalling that originally the ideograms for yin and yang stood for sunlight shining on a mountain, we draw closer to understanding where yin and yang reside in the psyche. Yin stood for the dark side of the mountain; yang, for the light side. What was it that caused these differentiations of light and shade? The sun. Because the sun is pure undifferentiated energy and its existence causes the distinction of light and shade, we have an allegorical picture of the supreme ultimate and the yin and yang differentiated out of it. As the sun causes the distinction of light and shade to be known, so too did the supreme ultimate cause yin and yang to come into existence. This coincides with the allusions contained in the above-mentioned quotes: There is the supreme ultimate as mind standing above and beyond a frame of immediate reference, and there is mind, human mind, composed of the two qualities that were separated out of original mind. This is what Wang Chung meant when he said that man carried the fluid of heaven and earth within him, and that that fluid is mind. Because yin and yang are often referred to in Chinese metaphysical thought as fluids, the statement made is that the unity of mind is made up of the dichotomy of yin and yang.

The mountain in our little allegorical example is composed of earth and stone. In contrast to light and shade, it is substantial. Rooted in earth, it reaches into the heavens. In ar-

chetypal language, the mountain is always understood as residing at the center of the earth, and the earth is known as
representing the human body. We therefore have the image
of the human body, or an aspect of the human body, with
sunlight on it. Its centrality points to the idea of an "I" or
"me," the ego. The yin and yang qualities are its two aspects:
the unconscious and conscious.

In the *Book of Changes* the yang quality as heaven is
power, energy, and motion. Its most important expression in
both world and universe is its creative mobility. It is outgoing, grasping, and perceiving, like consciousness. Earth
complements this active and creative principle. It is therefore
understood as the epitome of devotion. The creative and
heavenly principle causes things to come into being, but the
receptive and earthly principle gives birth to them. The masculine is spirit, the feminine, form.

The Oriental came to regard the interplay of these opposites as that found between husband and wife. Their coming
together caused children to be born possessing the qualities of
their parents. In other words, the children or components
born of the marriage of yang-consciousness and yin-uncon-
scious are further differentiations of the psyche.

The Family and Their Movements

The single yin or yang line in a trigram determines its sex.
A single yin line indicates that the trigram represents one of
the three daughters; a single yang, one of the sons. The position of the line, counting from the bottom up, reveals the age
of the child. Therefore:

The three sons speak of the three stages of movement; the
three daughters, of the three stages of quiescent devotion.
Within these six stages all human action may be defined.

Chên, the first son, is thunder and represents the beginning
of movement.

K'an, the second son, is water and represents danger in
movement.

Kên, the third son, is the mountain and represents the end
of movement.

Sun, the first daughter, is wind and wood and represents
the gentle but penetrating aspect of devotion.

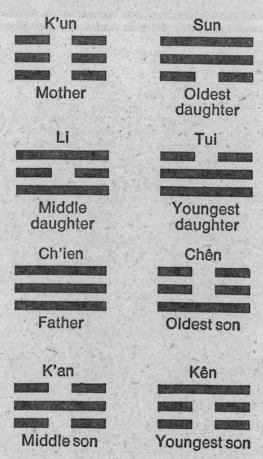

K'un

Mother

Sun

Oldest
daughter

Li

Middle
daughter

Tui

Youngest
daughter

Ch'ien

Father

Chên

Oldest son

K'an

Middle son

Kên

Youngest son

Li, the second daughter, is fire and represents clarity and adaptability.

Tui, the third daughter, is the lake and represents joyous tranquillity.

Each trigram has its own specific movement aside from those specifically referring us to the stages of change, as outlined above. The relevance of these movements will probably not be fully understood until we discuss the symbolic significations of the trigrams, but it is imperative we discuss their movements before we reach that section. We shall begin with the sons.

The movement of Chên is upward. Although its primary signification is thunder, it is often referred to as a blade of grass pushing its way up through the earth. Because it is the trigram of beginnings—as we shall see when we discuss the movement of the primal sequence below—it also refers us to the "upward" movement of time.

Chên is also a road. Its major movement being upward, one may mistakenly accept it to always signify movement up a road or a hill. Such is the case in Hexagram 27, The Corners of the Mouth. There we find the following image:

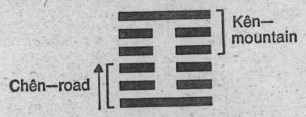

This is a road leading up to a mountain's summit. The hexagram's lines specifically indicate that the movement is upward, that the road leads from the bottom to the top. We find a different situation in Hexagram 62, Preponderance of the Small, where, although the lines do not themselves make mention of a road, the judgment states that one should not strive upward but should remain below. The picture is of a road on top of a mountain:

The only possible movement such a road could afford would be downward—hence, the advice that one should remain below, that one should not allow oneself to reach the height a bird does. The movement signification of the trigram has been modified. It is here employed to state that one should *not* move upward.

K'an

The movement of K'an is that of water, downward. Again, the movement of the trigram is actually determined by the trigram it accompanies. Therefore, in Hexagram 5, Waiting, we find all movement held in check in the form of clouds. The beneficent aspect of water has not yet been released. Here, water is regarded as nourishment. Its association with heaven, the fact that it will have to pass through the spiritual principle in order to descend, makes of it mana, food for the spirit.

Water or clouds

Heaven or sky

In Hexagram 7, The Army, we find water conserved beneath the earth.

Earth above

Water below

It has reached its level and is now in a state of conservation, increasing through inaction. In a state of stasis, water in this instance eventually becomes symbolic of strength in reserve.

This attribute comes from its association with the element earth, for earth gives form and substance to that which has none.

In Hexagram 47, Oppression, the image of the lake over water gives us the picture of an empty lake, its water buried deep in the earth.

Hexagram #47—Oppression

In Number 7, mentioned above, water contained within the earth is a sign of strength; but here, where water should be, it is not. Here it is not a matter of conservation of energy—it is a matter of a situation having been drained of all its energy, of its substance. There is no buildup of water mentioned. It truly stands still, indicating that it may soon become spoiled.

In Hexagram 3, Difficulty at the Beginning, the downward tendency of the trigram is coupled with the downward movement of two other trigrams to express difficulty: Both the nuclear trigrams Kên and K'un have downward movements in that they *press* downward. Theirs is more a signification of weight:

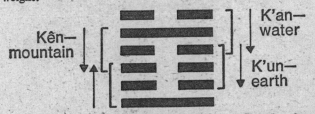

Hexagram #3—Difficulty at the Beginning

This oppressive weight bearing down on a blade of grass struggling to be born is accentuated by the idea that the downward tendency of the two trigrams, Kên and K'un, is actually a movement, not just a sinking. The idea of this movement is given by the trigram K'an standing above the three.

In Number 48, water has again found its level. Its upward movement is achieved by man's efforts. Here the nourishing aspect promised in Number 5 is present, but the nourishment is achieved only by an expenditure of energy.

In Number 8, Holding Together, the idea that water is standing still is even stronger: it is coupled with the nuclear trigram Kên, the trigram of keeping still. The water does not penetrate the earth, it stands above it.

Hexagram #8—Holding Together

This idea is stated again by the nuclear trigram Kên. Water on the top of the mountain does not move, as we are told in Number 39, Obstruction. Therefore, the trigram Kên in this instance is used as a modifier to tell us that the water in this instance does not penetrate, does not move downward.

In Hexagram 60, Limitation, the picture is of water moving upward:

Hexagram #60—Limitation

As in Hexagrams 7 and 39, water reverses its natural movement by accumulating. In this hexagram such a movement is considered negative in that no limits have been set to the situation. In Number 39, Obstruction, there has been an

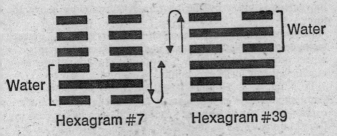

Water

Water

Hexagram #7   Hexagram #39

overemphasis on limitation; therefore, the upward movement is a positive one. In Number 7, The Army, it too is positive because it represents a conservation of energy.

The only hexagram in which water moves upward of its own accord is Number 4, Youthful Folly, where we have the image of water as a spring at the foot of a mountain.

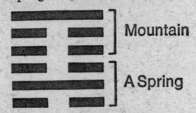

Mountain

A Spring

Hexagram #4—Youthful folly

The advice given there is that an individual should be as a flowing spring, always moving and giving of himself.

I have purposefully spent a considerable amount of time on the various movements of this trigram in certain hexagrams to emphasize to the reader the fact that no signification a trigram might have should be considered as static and fixed. This trigram in particular bears that point out. In the discussion of the remaining trigrams, this should be kept in mind; the reader should refer to the hexagrams containing the specific trigram in order to see the modification and amplifications it undergoes in different situations.

Kên

The movement of Kên is downward. In this trigram, however, the movement must be regarded as more of a weighting or pressing down than either a mechanical or natural movement. In this regard, Kên must be thought of as a heaviness or excessiveness. In Hexagram 23, Splitting Apart, the weight is so excessive that it causes the roof of a house to fall in:

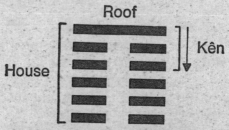

Hexagram #23—Splitting Apart

The weight of this trigram comes from its attribute of keeping still. When one keeps still, weight is concentrated at one point. If it is in the form of a mountain, the weight comes about because of an accumulation. In the above hexagram, the accumulation has reached its limit.

In Hexagram 41, the weight is a necessity and is used to contain an emotion, the joyousness of the lower trigram, Tui:

Hexagram #41—Decrease

Here the trigram takes on a moral aspect to become a restraining force.

The movement of Sun is upward. Because this trigram has two major significations assigned it, wind and wood, the reader who finds it in a hexagram should determine which of the two significations is more prominently displayed in that instance.

In Hexagram 53, Development, we are presented with the image of a tree on a mountain:

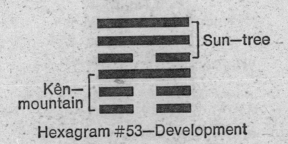

Hexagram #53—Development

But in Hexagram 20, Contemplation, we are given the image of the wind blowing over the face of the earth:

Hexagram #20—Contemplation

In this hexagram the movement of the trigram is more an outspreading than an upward movement. It is an obvious movement in this instance. If one considers the trigram's attribute of wood carefully, one also finds the outspreading movement there—slower and imperceptible, but definitely outspreading.

In Hexagram 46, Pushing Upward, the movement of this trigram is clearly upward. The image is of wood pushing its way up through the earth:

Hexagram #46—Rushing Upward

The outspreading, diffuse movement of this trigram will be discussed further when we turn to the additional attributes of this and the other trigrams. For the time being, view the trigram as having a predominantly upward-moving tendency.

The movement of fire is upward. In Hexagram 21 this trigram's movement is somewhat modified. As the hexagram's upper trigram, it represents the upper portion of a mouth; the lower trigram, Chên, represents the bottom portion. The action spoken of is that of biting:

Hexagram #21—Biting Through

In this hexagram we have an excellent example of one of the many ways a trigram's movements may be modified. It will be noticed that all the trigrams we have discussed in terms of movement are present. The trigram K'an is found as the upper nuclear trigram, the trigram Kên as the lower nuclear trigram:

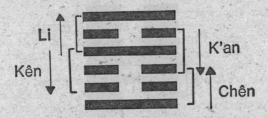

Fire, by its very nature, can know only one movement, but here we find the trigram held somewhat in check. True, the upper portion of a mouth moves, but its movement takes place within a fixed space. The presence of a trigram with so strong a predominance for upward movement in a place signifying that which is above—the upper three places of a hexagram standing for that which is above—would seem to accentuate the trigram's nature. Much the same could be said for the lower primary trigram, Chên. The trigram not only represents movement, but movement of considerable force. It is fitting that this trigram was deciphered as representing the lower jaw. Both trigrams, however, are considerably modified in that they are set within an image, that of a mouth, whose movement is more a tendency than an expression of the natural and spontaneous movement brought to mind by these two trigrams. Here, we are to see one of the functions of the nuclear trigrams.

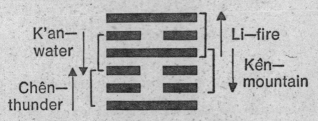

Fire is pulled down by water;
thunder is held down by mountain

It is to be noticed that the upper nuclear trigram is K'an, or water—that which by its very nature seeks its own level by a downward movement.

The primary trigram Li, fire, is literally held by this water trigram. Because fire and water are the most antagonistic of the elements and therefore excellent symbols for the opposites, one can easily envision here a state of tension. This state speaks to us of an ability to move up and down. The movement of the fire trigram, strong as it is, has been modified by the water trigram, whose equally insistent downward movement causes the upper trigram at times to move down.

The lower nuclear trigram Kên, the mountain, sits on top of the powerful thunder trigram, Chên. Again, a strong upward-moving tendency is held check by an equally strong downward movement.

If the fourth and yang line of this hexagram were a yin line, we would have Hexagram 27, The Corners of the Mouth:

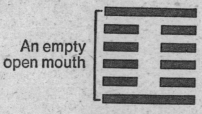

An empty
open mouth

Hexagram #27—
The Corners of the Mouth

In that hexagram the picture is of an open mouth. Here, in Hexagram 21, we are told that an obstruction is present that does not allow the lips to come together. Hence the necessity of biting through the obstruction. The nuclear hexagrams in this instance shed further light. The lower nuclear hexagram is Hexagram 27, The Corners of the Mouth. Atop it is the primary nuclear hexagram, Number 39, Obstruction, pressing down on the open mouth.

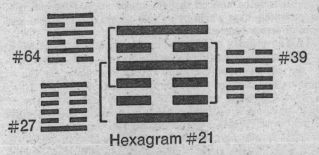

#64

#27

#39

Hexagram #21

The upper nuclear hexagram is Hexagram 64, Before Completion, in which we are told that the time of disorder is not yet over. In Hexagram 21, Biting Through, therefore, we are referred to a situation demanding that we achieve union by energetically putting things in order. The ideogram for this hexagram literally translates into "union by gnawing." When one receives this hexagram, one should take into consideration the primary nuclear hexagram of Obstruction. Actually, a look at every hexagram's primary nuclear hexagram is instructive. In this hexagram we have an exceptionally clear visual statement.

Tui

The movement of Tui is downward. The downward tendency of this trigram is fully expressed in Hexagram 47, Oppression. There the trigram, in its attribute of lake, is shown drained of its water:

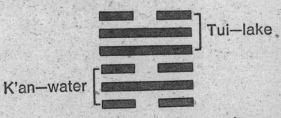

Tui—lake

K'an—water

Hexagram #47—Oppression

Because of its attribute of lake the trigram sometimes is used to express the idea of a gathering toward a center and contained space, as in Hexagram 45, Gathering Together, where we are presented with the image of water gathering over one point on the surface of the earth:

Hexagram #45—Gathering Together

Often, however, this trigram is spoken of as moving outward. This occurs in those instances where the trigram's attribute of mouth is being employed, as in Hexagram 58, The Joyous.

Because Ch'ien and K'un will be analyzed in detail when we discuss the significations, we will only mention here that the former has an upward movement, the latter a downward movement.

The Attributes

Each trigram has been assigned a number of symbolic attributes. The reader should make every effort to memorize these because they are the key to hexagram interpretation.

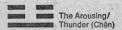

The Arousing/
Thunder (Chên)

This is the trigram of movement. Its animal is the dragon. In the human body, it manifests itself in the foot. Its color is dark yellow. It is symbolic of the act of laying or spreading out. It is a great road, an eldest son. It is decisive and vehement. It is bamboo that is green and young. It is reed and rush. It is a horse that neighs well, and it also stands for horses with white hind legs, good prancers and gallopers, and those with white stars on their foreheads. In the plant world it symbolizes that which returns to life after its disappearance beneath the surface of the earth. It represents that in the vegetable kingdom which is strong and grows luxuriantly.

This trigram is the first or eldest son of the family of trigrams and represents the beginning of movement. It is the trigram of energy and power, spontaneity and decisiveness. Here resides one of the negative aspects of this trigram, for spontaneity easily lends itself to recklessness, action without thought.

According to the ancient Chinese, thunder is caused by yang fluid exploding. This comes about, we are told, because of the compression of yin and yang fluids. What we have here is an instance of the clashing of the opposites, of two opposing views or ways of being. The sound of thunder announces the beginning of a new movement, the opening of another passage. Because it is the sign for beginnings as well as the trigram that initiates the moment of creation in the sequence of early heaven, we should look at it within the hexagram that speaks of beginnings: Number 3, Difficulty at the Beginning.

The sequence for this hexagram tells us that after heaven and earth came into existence individual things began to develop; this hexagram speaks of the circumstances surrounding that moment. As we mentioned in the chapter on the hexagrams, this third hexagram of the *Book of Changes* is the "child" of the two hexagrams preceding it. Chên, the first child to be born of this union, is here pictured in the womb of his mother, the trigram K'un:

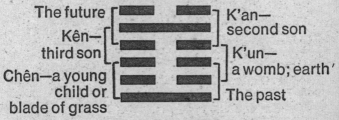

Hexagram #3—
Difficulty at the Beginning

You will also notice that the other two sons, K'an and Kên, are present. Whereas the first son is in the section of the hexagram signifying the past, the lower, thereby indicating that he is oldest in time, the two brothers are above and in the future. The visual sequence of the book makes its first statement: True devotion, represented by the mother trigram K'un, is not fruitless. The child born of this meeting of heaven and earth is represented as at first being weak. The ideogram for this hexagram presents us with the picture of a plant or blade of grass struggling to penetrate the surface of the earth.

What element in the hexagram diagrams difficulty? The trigram K'an has as its major movement-signification that of danger in movement or, as modified by the situation depicted in this hexagram, difficulty of movement. The trigram we are here discussing, Chên, is the trigram of movement and is representative of the foot. That the trigram for danger or difficulty, K'an, stands above the trigram for movement implies, if not explicitly states, that there is difficulty and danger in this present attempt at movement.

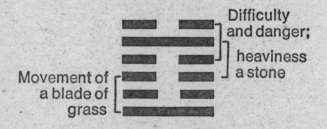

Difficulty and danger; heaviness a stone

Movement of a blade of grass

The tension and difficulty of the moment comes not only from the downward movement of K'an, but also from the oppressive weight of the upper nuclear trigram Kên, the Mountain. Add to this the fact that the downward movement of the lower nuclear trigram K'un demands that the young Chên as a blade of grass force its way through it, and you have a satisfactory picture of difficulty. Kên, we shall discover when we discuss its attributes below, is also a stone. The blade of grass, Chên, not only must push itself up through the earth, but must also contend with a heavy

(K'an) stone (Kên). The hexagram not only speaks of the
difficulty the thing to be born encounters, but also of the
thing that gives birth, K'un, the earth. It must contain, but
only to the point where it is not oppressive. It is a difficult
undertaking and one that most certainly demands true devotion, as the trigram for the mother, K'un, represents. In that
the trigram refers us to the idea of beginnings and birth, it
speaks of the thunder, strength, and affect which usually accompanies new ideas or attitudes. Therefore, this hexagram
shows us the early stages of such births—their dangers and re-
wards.

Another important aspect of this trigram, Chên, is its
sound. It is the sound of thunder—pure, undifferentiated
sound, the sound of Nature. In its original form this sound is
disordered. True, thunder is awe inspiring, but, perhaps for
that very reason, it does not cause one to lean toward it. In
its beginnings, the *Book of Changes* tells us, sound comes
rumbling out of the earth. It is chaotic and expressive of difficulties. By the time we reach Hexagram 16, Enthusiasm, we
find a different tale.

The enthusiasm has to do with the fact that the blade of
grass buried in the earth in Hexagram 3 is here shown as
having arrived at the surface:

Chên is the trigram of spring, of beginnings in nature,
when what had retreated during winter returns. The difficulty
spoken of in Hexagram 3 has been surmounted. What was
chaotic has now become harmonious. What has grown to its
fullest potential is in harmony with the laws of the universe.
The sound of thunder, the essence of sound itself, is here attended to by the devoted (K'un) hand (Kên). Pure sound,
sound without form, has been given form (K'un). The nuclear trigram Kên refers to the idea that a prerequisite for
harmony is the knowledge that when something has become

fully developed it is time to keep still, time to pause and rest.

To show just how full a story each hexagram offers it is profitable to analyze this hexagram a bit further.

The text appended to this hexagram, The Image, tells us that the time imaged here is one when kings make music. The music is being played on a flute or other wind instrument. The trigram Kên has as its body attribute the hand and fingers; the trigram K'an has assigned it the quality of penetration, the ability to make holes. Therefore, the piece of bamboo (Chên) which the hand (Kên) holds has holes (made by K'an) in it upon which the fingers (Kên) rest:

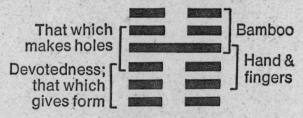

In the diagram of early heaven, thunder gives rise to wind —this is the wind passing through the flute. Another image that immediately presents itself is that of a foot dancing on the earth:

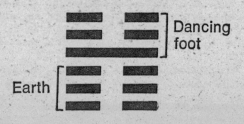

The primary upper trigram Chên has an upward movement; the upper nuclear trigram, K'an, of which Chên is a part, has a downward movement. This up and down movement associated with the image of a foot speaks quite simply of rhythm and dancing.

Further attributes of Chên are: a general, a ruler, music, agitation, work, and voices.

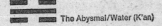 The Abysmal/Water (K'an)

The abysmal is water and danger. Its animal is the pig. In the human body, it manifests itself in the ear. It's color is blood-red. It is the symbol for channels and ditches, draining and irrigation. It speaks of that which is hidden and concealed. It is used when one wishes to express the idea of either bending or straightening out. It is a bow and a wheel. In man, it refers to the condition of melancholy and anxiety, distress and uncertainty. It is blood and a man with an earache. In referring to horses it suggests the idea of those with strong and elegant backs, those with courage, those with dropping heads, and those with thin hoofs who stumble. It is a broken-down carriage. It is that which penetrates. It is the moon. It means thieves. As a tree, it is one that is strong and has much pith.

Because it is the trigram of thieves, it also speaks of deceit. In Hexagram 29, The Abysmal, the hexagram made up of K'an doubled, reference is made to the fact that the trigram also stands for thorns and prisons.

In Hexagram 39, Obstruction, we find another attribute—that of difficulty. The ideogram for this hexagram translates into "incompetent feet and legs causing difficulty in walking." The lower primary trigram is Kên, the trigram of keeping still; the upper nuclear trigram is Li, one of whose attributes is activity. This activity is hemmed in on both sides by K'an, whose attribute of imprisonment is significant in this instance. Activity has been brought to a dead halt. (See p. 106)

Another attribute of the upper nuclear trigram, Li, is the crab. This too is suggestive of how great the obstruction is: Things have been slowed down to the pace of a crab.

Imprisonment and difficulty

A crab

Non-movement

Hexagram #39—Obstruction

Because K'an stands for blood and water, the top line of Hexagram 3, Difficulty at the Beginning, finds its source in this trigram. The trigram's attributes of blood, water, and downward movement are referred to at one time to form one image—that of bloody tears.

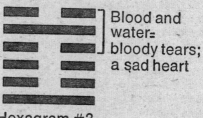

Blood and water= bloody tears; a sad heart

Hexagram #3— Difficulty at the Beginning

Because the trigram is here used to symbolize tears, it gains the further attribute of sadness, if not pain. This seems to be in accord with its attribute of heart and all that pertains to the heart, especially its experience of sorrow. Again, in Hexagram 3, lines two, four, and six, we find mention of a horse and a wagon, which are attributes of the trigram.

The quality of penetration is also assigned this trigram. The same quality is assigned the trigram Sun, but in that trigram, feminine by nature, penetration is gentle. K'an—masculine, forceful, and in motion—speaks of penetration as an act of force and violence. In the trigram Sun, the penetration is that of growing things and occurs within a field of gentleness and devotion. In K'an the decisiveness and activity of the male is the determining factor. In Hexagram 48, line two, we find the image of a leaking jug. A jug is one of the significations assigned the upper nuclear trigram, Li. The fact that the jug leaks indicates it has holes in it. The presence of the holes is further suggested by the upper primary trigram K'an, that which penetrates or makes holes.

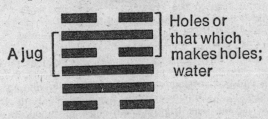

Holes or that which makes holes; water

A jug

Hexagram #48—The Well

Furthermore, the trigram K'an in Hexagram 48, The Well, stands not only for the holes in the jug, but also for the water that leaks out of it. The point to be brought out here is that all attributes of a trigram are applicable when the situation calls for them. Just because we use one particular attribute of a trigram to explain a line or an answer does not mean that the trigram then becomes a static figure. If the situation depicted by the hexagram allows, any and all significations may be brought into the picture.

For example, other attributes of the trigram K'an are moistness, clouds, obtuseness, meat and drink, order, wisdom, oracle, darkness, fear, cunning, worry, wine, and soul.

Keeping Still /
Mountain (Kên)

Keeping Still is the mountain. It is a mountain path and small stones, doors and other openings of any type. Its animal is the dog, which keeps still in order to protect and guard. It is also the rat, and symbolizes birds with powerful black bills. As a tree, it is strong and gnarled. It is a fruit and the seed of a fruit. In the human body, it manifests itself in the hand and its fingers. It is a porter or a watchman, and a eunuch.

Because Kên represents the end of all movement it also speaks of the time when things have reached their fullest development. In the top line of Hexagram 23, Splitting Apart, we find this trigram standing for a large uneaten fruit. That it is about to fall off the tree of its own weight indicates that it has reached its complete development. Here, in the image of fruit, we have yet another attribute—that of rebirth. When the fruit falls to the ground and dies, the seeds contained within it cause the cycle of growth to begin again. Therefore, the time of Splitting Apart is immediately followed by Hexagram 24, Return. There we see that the trigram Kên, which has fallen to the ground as fruit, has now become the trigram Chen, a small seedling pushing its way up through the earth.

In Hexagram 52, Keeping Still, which is composed of Kên doubled, we are told that things cannot be in continuous motion. One must make them stop. "Making things stop" once they have achieved their end speaks of conscious effort. The trigram also symbolizes the hand, further underlining the idea of a purposeful directing of will—one literally takes things in hand, for it is the hand that allows us to grasp and hold things, to restrain and restrict the movement and progression of things.

Because Kên also stands for eunuchs, watchmen, and dogs, it refers us to the idea of standing watch over a situation. A eunuch is a sexless being originally used to guard the women's quarters against male intruders. This would seem to suggest, as does the text accompanying Hexagram 52, Keeping Still, that the trigram speaks of the necessity at times of quieting, stilling the passions.

Further attributes of Kên are a house, forest, a hostel or hotel, inner reserve, and clarity.

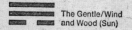 The Gentle/Wind and Wood (Sun)

The Gentle penetrates as does wood and wind. Its animal is the cock. In the human body it manifests itself in the thighs. Its color is white. It is a plumb line and a carpenter's square. It is that which is long, that which is high. It is the trigram of advance and retreat; therefore, it is also the sign of indecisiveness. It is odor. It is men with balding or gray hair, men with wide foreheads, men with much white in their eyes. It signifies the pursuit of gain. It is the sign of vehemence.

Because this is the trigram that breaks up the winter ice imprisoning the yang principle, it is thought of as giving form to things. For this reason it is also a trigram of work and toil.

In contrast to its brother, Chên, which speaks of decisive movement, this trigram in its aspect of wind is the epitome of indecisiveness and doubt. We find an excellent example of this attribute in line four of Hexagram 31, Influence. Here we are presented with the picture of a man agitated in mind, his thoughts going to and fro. His mind is represented by Ch'ien, Heaven; his indecisiveness by Sun:

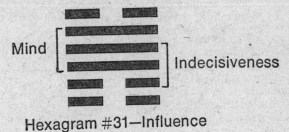

Hexagram #31—Influence

In Part II, Chapter 5 of the appendix to the *Book of Changes,* "Discussion of the Trigrams," we are told that this line portrays the penetration of a germinal thought into the mind. The germinal thought and the mind are represented by Ch'ien; the penetration of the thought is represented by the trigram Sun:

This commentary is a further indication that the diagram of Earlier Heaven was understood as a diagram outlining the process of the human mind—the process of the spirit Tao or supreme ultimate as consciousness.

Further attributes of the trigram Sun are a bond, riches,

money, fellowship, property, fish, concealment, a wood, a thicket.

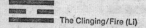

The Clinging/Fire (LI)

The Clinging means dependence. Its animal is the pheasant or firebird. It also signifies the turtle, crab, snail, mussel, and tortoise. In the human body, it manifests itself in the eye and in men with large bellies. It is the sun. It is a coat of mail and a helmet, a spear and a sword. It is dry. As a tree, it is hollow and rotten at the top.

In contrast to the second brother, K'an, which is water and signifies moistness, this trigram is fire and signifies that which is dry. In Hexagram 21, Biting Through, the image of old dried meat is derived from this attribute.

Because of its brilliance as fire and sun, this trigram is associated with the clarity of consciousness. In accordance with its fiery aspect, it is understood to be a sign of tenacity, arising out of the phenomenon of a flame's appearance of clinging to the substance it feeds on. This is the reason why in Hexagram 54, The Marrying Maiden, it is said the female follows and clings to the man:

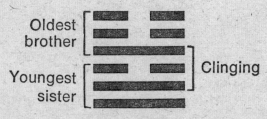

Oldest brother

Youngest sister

Clinging

Hexagram #54—The Marrying Maiden

This trigram is also symbolic of the eye. In Hexagram 30, The Clinging, line five, we find reference to a flood of tears. You will notice that the upper nuclear trigram, Tui, the lake, is enmeshed with this trigram. Tui's movement is downward—hence, a flood of tears:

A lake

An eye

Hexagram #30—The Clinging

The trigram's attribute of weapons is borne out in Hexagram 36, Darkening of the Light, in which the theme of wounding frequently occurs. In this hexagram Li is coupled with the lower nuclear trigram K'an, the trigram which in its dangerous aspect penetrates. In this hexagram we are told that the dark force injures the light force.

Further attributes of Li are form, order, enlightened will, beauty and lightning.

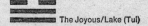 The Joyous/Lake (Tui)

The Joyous is a lake, a low-lying collection of water, a marsh. The Joyous means pleasure. Its animal is the sheep. In the human body, it manifests itself in the mouth. It is a sorceress, she who speaks wise words. It is the tongue. It is the trigram of decay and of dropping down and bursting open. It is hard and salty soil. It is a concubine.

I would like at this time to discuss Hexagram 54, The Marrying Maiden, which contains this trigram. Of all hexagrams in the *Book of Changes,* Number 54 seems most to defy interpretation. I offer here a possible explanation and will show how some of the attributes of the trigram Tui are employed.

The name of the hexagram, Kuei Mei, literally means returning and younger sister, or the return of the younger sister. The younger sister is Tui, which is in back and follows close on the heels of the elder brother, Chên.

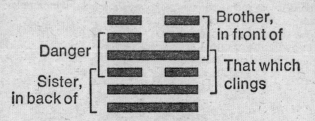

Brother, in front of

Danger

That which clings

Sister, in back of

Hexagram #54—The Marrying Maiden

You will notice that the trigram Tui, the younger sister, is enmeshed with the trigram Li, the Clinging. Also notice that the Clinging has a dangerous aspect to it in that Li is in turn enmeshed with the nuclear trigram K'an, the trigram of danger. The sister's affection for her brother, her clinging to him, is fraught with danger and bodes disaster.

Line six of this hexagram reveals what its time refers to: the time of sacrifice. The source of this line is a text of the Chou, Chin, and Han dynasties (480–202 B.C.), and reads:

When the Son of Heaven performs the great sacrifice and the suburban sacrifice,* he must himself shoot the sacrificial victims, and his queen must herself pound the sacrificial grain. The feudal lords when they perform their ancestral sacrifices, must themselves shoot the ox, stab the sheep, and kill the pig, and their consorts must themselves pound the grain for the vessels . . . It is through the sacrifices that the unity of the people is strengthened. [quoted in Fung Yu-lan, *A History of Chinese Philosophy*, Vol. I]

Generally speaking, during the time of sacrifice the trans-personal and the mundane become united. In other words, it is the moment of the union of the opposites. In our hexagram

---

* The suburban sacrifice was one performed in the suburbs on two occasions during the year. In winter, the sacrifice was performed in honor of heaven; in summer, in honor of earth. Its purpose was to express gratitude toward the originators and recall beginnings.

in the nuclear trigrams K'an and Li, we have visually recorded just such a moment. The symbol most often employed to portray the union of the opposites is that of the marriage of the sun and moon. Li is the sun, K'an the moon. These two trigrams also represent the sacrificial knife (Li) and the blood of the sacrifice (K'an).

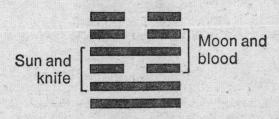

Sun and knife

Moon and blood

To all appearances, the elements necessary for a successful sacrifice are present, but the text accompanying the top line tells us that when the man stabs the sheep no blood flows, and the basket the woman holds is empty. The fruits of the harvest are not in the basket, and the sheep is without blood, without soul. The *Li Chi*, or *Book of Rites*, tells us that the suburban sacrifice was performed to express gratitude toward the originators and to recall the beginnings of man and the universe. The sacrifice is not something that comes from without; rather, it is born in the heart and offered in all sincerity and good faith. In other words, the participants of such a moment must have all their attention focused on the sacred event if it is to be efficacious. Such is not the case in this hexagram. The ritual, according to line six, has failed. In order to find the cause of this failure it will be necessary to investigate the nature of the individuals performing the sacrifice.

The upper primary trigram, Chên, the older brother, is truly involved in venerating heaven: the upper two lines of the trigram occupy the two places assigned heaven in a trigram. His every action, however, takes place in the heart of danger, the two lower lines of this trigram being enmeshed with the upper primary trigram, K'an, the trigram of danger.

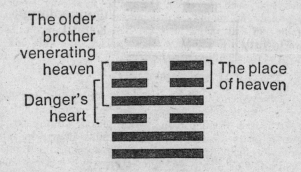

The lower primary trigram, Tui, the younger sister, not only follows close behind but is busy talking—Tui stands for the mouth and Chên (as revealed in Hexagram 21) for the voice. The lower nuclear trigram Li has an attribute of cleverness assigned to it. Therefore, the words that come out of the sister's mouth are clever words:

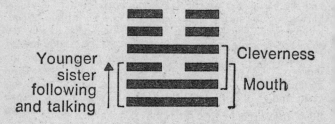

The upper nuclear trigram K'an stands not only for danger but also for thieves and for pits in which things may be concealed. It is the trigram of concealment and theft. The words that come out of the sister's mouth are not only clever, they are also hidden—lies—and they are being used to steal (K'an) something. Not only is Tui gay and beautiful (Li), but so also are her words, and therefore all the more deceptive.

The movement of the lower nuclear trigram Li has been brought to a standstill by the combined movements of the upper nuclear trigram K'an, which presses down, and the lower primary trigram Tui, which pulls down. In other words, the lightning (Li) that usually accompanies thunder (Chên) and the clarity of vision (Li), which is needed during the time of beginnings (Chên), is being suppressed.

The total picture is of a beautiful young maiden with a lovely voice and enticing manner who with the aid of sweet but deceptive words attempts to attract the masculine principle away from his task. As a concubine she is capable of convincing the male that no harm will come to him if he stays and tarries awhile with her. But the hexagram tells us that union with her will only bring misfortune. She is trying to steal the union of the opposites, the marriage of sun and moon, heaven and earth, for her own ends. This figure of the enticing but dangerous maiden appears time and again in fairy tales. She is Calypso who entices and ensnares the hero Odysseus; the lady of the fountain who causes the knight to forget his search for the Grail. In short, she is the enchantress who always manifests herself to the hero and attempts to keep him from his task. She is the dark and feminine P'o soul the Chinese claim is contained within each of us—the force that continually attempts to swallow and devour the light and active principle of consciousness.

Chên stands here as a newborn thought or attitude in dan-

ger of being drawn back down into the abyss of nonreason,
or being sucked back down into the center of the lake where
a harmless-looking mermaid beckons and prepares a trap.
The general statement the hexagram makes is that we are
being enticed into a dangerous condition; that a new attitude,
realization, or way of life is being threatened by The Marrying Maiden. On the whole, the time is not the proper one
for a movement toward the feminine principle. In her present
aspect, she brings more chance of misfortune than success. A
proper relationship with the feminine principle is possible,
but in this hexagram there is only one instance in which this
condition exists. The text accompanying line five indicates
that the maiden has attained the position of a princess. In the
sense that Tui stands for a sorceress, she brings to the active
male principle oracles and intuitions to aid him in his quest.

Further attributes of Tui are that which is lowest, magician, calendar maker, white tiger, number and gaiety.

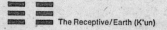 The Receptive/Earth (K'un)

This is the trigram of docility. Its animal is the cow. In the
human body it manifests itself in the belly. It is the earth and
the mother. It is cloth, a cauldron, a kettle, or a large wagon.
It is level. It is a cow with a young heifer. It is that which
gives form to things, or form itself. It is the multitude, a
shaft. It is black soil.

The major attribute of this trigram is devoted gentleness.
K'un complements its opposite, Ch'ien, the Creative. The
statement it makes is that the proper application of strength
should be one motivated by gentleness. True strength is gentle; true gentleness, by the same token, is not an insipid re-
ceptiveness, a falling back or cowardly refusal to take action,
but rather an ability to be receptive to all that one is confronted with.

During the first century A.D., the *Book of Changes* began
to be employed as a manual of alchemy. The first two hexagrams of the book, Heaven and Earth, stood for the chemical
apparatus. The hexagram named after and composed of this
trigram, K'un, was understood to be the vessel in which
things were placed to be transformed. This idea probably
arose from the trigram's attribute of a kettle. Alchemical lit-

erature throughout the centuries has always spoken of this vessel as uterus or womb. So also, this trigram refers us to the image of the earth as womb in which all things are contained, from which they sprout, and to which they return. When we discuss the movement of the sequence of early heaven we will discover that this trigram is associated with the season of winter, during which time the active yang principle, which had caused things to sprout in spring, takes shelter. Hexagram 23, Splitting Apart, speaks of this event. The dark earth principle, black soil being an attribute of this trigram, forces the light and creative principle from the world, but takes it into itself and shelters it until the time of its return.

It is important to keep in mind the fact that the receptive principle must be activated and lead by the creative yang principle. If ignored, the dark force seeks to gain entry into the world by force and to supplant the light. Here is seen the destructive aspect of the trigram. Because one of its attributes is a cloth or blanket—that which covers, warms, and protects —we may also speak of the trigram's ability to smother and imprison.

Because K'un is the trigram standing for form, it speaks of completing what has been begun, of giving form to creative ideas. It accomplishes this through gentle devotion. Because it represents the multitude, it also stands for a nation. Further attributes of K'un are a wall, frugality, a city, a ritual vessel.

 The Creative/
Heaven (Ch'ien)

Ch'ien is the trigram of strength. Its animal is the horse. It is a good horse, an old horse, a thin horse, a wild horse. In the human body, it manifests itself in the head. It is a ruler or prince, a father. It is round, a circle. It is cool jade. It is cold and ice. Its color is red. It is the fruit of trees.

This trigram's attribute of strength should in no way be thought of as force, but rather as the strength that causes things to endure. This trigram represents constancy, duration in time. Because it is formless, its strength is not seen, but makes its presence known by its effect. Because it is heaven it also refers us to the concept of infinite space. The major quality of this trigram is, therefore, duration in time and space. The Creative principle is strong because its effects are everlasting. In matters of personality transformation, this trigram refers us to the strength of being which, although supportive of the entire personality, does not force notice of its presence. The negative aspect of this trigram manifests itself in obstinacy, hardness, and icy unemotionalism.

In its positive aspect, the Creative is that which impregnates, causes sudden insights. It is power, motion, energy, and the cause of time. Because of its roundness, it may be understood as representing totality, the totality of heaven.

In closing this section on the attributes of the trigrams, it is necessary to point out that when a changing line is present in a hexagram, and therefore in a trigram, the attributes of the trigram it is about to change into must often be considered along with those of the original trigram. To show how this moment amplifies or modifies the attribute of the original trigram (the trigram containing the changing line), the remainder of this section will be devoted to discussing the trigram Ch'ien as a changing trigram. We shall see how this trigram changes into the other seven, and what effects each change has on the original nature of the trigram.

Because it is the trigram standing for the head, it refers us to creative thought, active meditation. Its iciness refers us to cold rationalism. When the middle line is a changing line we have before us the image of the sun in heaven:

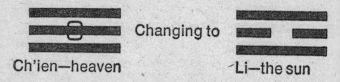

Ch'ien—heaven   Changing to   Li—the sun

The attribute of intelligence holds true in this instance, for the trigram Li stands not only for the sun, but also for the eye. These two significations refer us to perception: the sun illuminates and the eye sees. Therefore, the trigram Ch'ien, with a changing second line, would refer us to spirit manifesting itself as bright intelligence illuminating the world. Because Li is also a firebird, birds symbolically standing for the intuitive faculty of mind, the image of the firebird in heaven again points to illuminating intelligence. The firebird is a phoenix that rises up newly born out of its own ashes—a symbol of rebirth and duration in time. As the sun rises every day, so must the bright bird of consciousness always be present.

When the second and third lines of Ch'ien are in movement, the resulting trigram is Chên, The Arousing, Thunder:

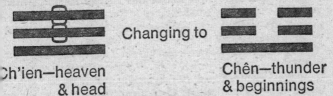

Changing to

Ch'ien—heaven
& head

Chên—thunder
& beginnings

Here, the attribute of movement is accentuated, for Chên is the first son, representing the beginning of movement. There is great strength here. The emergence of the spirit is thunderous. Because Chên is the first son, we are also referred to the idea of beginnings. The energy of Ch'ien is that of thunder, of flashes of lightning. The first picture that comes to mind now is that of enlightenment. An idea flashes in the head (Ch'ien) and spurs one to action. It is a fresh new idea bearing great strength. Chên is also the trigram of the foot; therefore we have the image of creative movement, movement with purpose.

When the first and third lines of Ch'ien are moving, the resulting trigram is K'an:

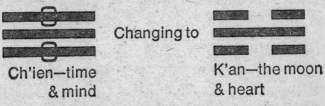

Changing to

Ch'ien—time
& mind

K'an—the moon
& heart

Here, the first fact to be noticed is that K'an is the moon, and that the attribute of time in Ch'ien becomes specific: The time is cyclic time, the time of the moon, of waxing and waning, of death and rebirth. The dangerous aspect of K'an (for K'an represents danger) has to do with surviving the effects of waxing and waning, of increase and decrease. But K'an also stands for the heart, and here we seem to have a union of heart and mind. The cold rational aspect of the consciousness is here given warmth and affection by K'an, the heart.

The image could very easily be that of a mind affectionately lingering over pleasant memories, or of a mind filled with emotion.

Because K'an also stands for danger in movement, it refers us to the idea that in order to move in the midst of danger one must have courage. Therefore, in the heart of danger one moves with strength and courage, or at least has courageous thoughts.

Let me again point out here that the images offered by the trigrams not only make statements about an existing condition, but may also be offering suggestions as to the proper course of action one should take. In the fourth and sixth lines of Hexagram 6, Conflict, which are also the first and third lines of the trigram Ch'ien, we see this point illustrated.

The fourth line indicates that one should not at this time engage in conflict, that it would be better to submit to one's fate and go back the way one came. To step back from a conflict and admit one's attitude is incorrect is most certainly a courageous and difficult move. However, to continue in a state of conflict would be to call up the dangerous aspect of the trigram K'an; by submitting to one's fate, moreover, one invokes the courageous energy of the trigram. Position and attitude are what determine which of a trigram's significations will have effect in an individual life. To go on in a situation of conflict would be to invite danger, to call forth the energy present in the trigram that would be injurious to the personality. By turning back, one causes the courageous attribute of K'an to manifest itself.

The sixth line bears this out, for there it is revealed that the individual has not taken the advice of the fourth line. He has gone ahead and supposedly won, only to be attacked again and again. The conflict continues and the individual finds himself in a constant state of danger. The fourth line offered a suggestion, the sixth line makes a statement. A hexagram sometimes tells us where we are in a situation on the one hand, and on the other, warns us what might happen if we do not take a new course of action.

Inasmuch as the trigram K'an also stands for thieves, it is the trigram of deceit. Another picture it gives us is of deceitful thought.

When the first and second line of Ch'ien are moving, the resulting trigram is Kên, the mountain:

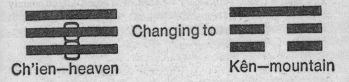

Ch'ien—heaven   **Kên—mountain**

Changing to

The mountain is the trigram of remaining still, the end of movement. The time aspect of Ch'ien is again modified: now it speaks of the end of a time, the cessation of movement. But the trigram Kên is also the trigram of autumn, the time when growing things reach their completion, their fullest potential. The seeds of the fruit are now fully developed, ready for future rebirth. The seed contains the tree itself and is therefore a receptacle of energy. Here, the image is also of great energy being stored up, piled as the stones and earth of a mountain. It is a very strong image. Ch'ien, which is shapeless spirit or energy, is here collected at one point and kept still, temporarily held in check, accumulated for its release in the spring.

When the first line of Ch'ien is in motion, the resulting trigram is Sun, the Gentle or Wind:

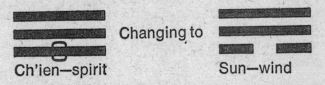

Ch'ien—spirit   **Sun—wind**

Changing to

This combination yields many statements, all of which may be upheld by a comparative analysis of the concept of spirit in other cultures throughout time. The trigram Sun is the trigram not only of wind, but of penetration. When it is combined with the Ch'ien signification of spirit, we have the image of a penetrating, impregnating spirit. On the other hand, the trigram Sun is that which, in the diagram of early heaven, breaks up the winter's ice. Therefore, because the trigram Ch'ien is ice, we find its aspect of being dissolved. Again, because wind moves about without purpose, Sun stands for indecisiveness. In combination with Ch'ien, it represents indecisiveness of mind. Because, as the wind, it is limitless, in combination with Ch'ien it refers us to the limit-lessness of time. At the same time, Sun is as formless as Ch'ien. The two in combination also point to the idea that nothing has developed as yet. The spirit or energy ranges about freely, unchecked and as yet useless.

When the upper line of Ch'ien is in movement the result-ing trigram is Tui, the lake:

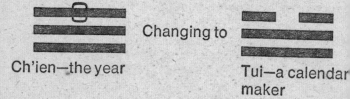

Ch'ien—the year   Changing to   Tui—a calendar maker

Of the many attributes assigned the trigram Tui, the one most significant is that of calendar maker. The calendar mak-ers of the Shang dynasty comprised the priest and magician caste. Here we are presented with Ch'ien as the year; spirit and its operations are regulated and recorded. Tui is also a sorceress who uses wise words when speaking with spirit. At the same time Tui stands for the act of falling and breaking apart, as a fruit falls from a tree and breaks when it hits the ground. The mind here is in danger of doing the same.

When all three lines of the Ch'ien trigram are in move-ment, the resulting trigram is K'un, the Receptive, its comple-ment:

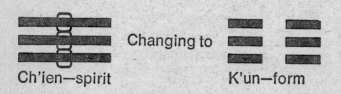

Ch'ien—spirit   Changing to   K'un—form

Here a complete reversal takes place. The Creative, that is, movement, has reached its pinnacle and gives its position over to the tranquillity and devotedness of the feminine prin-ciple.

We have just seen how the father trigram, Ch'ien, yields

the seven other trigrams. Each of the eight trigrams may yield the other seven. As we just witnessed in Ch'ien, the primary trigram in question, that is, the trigram containing the changing lines, is either modified or amplified by the trigram it changes into. The problem is of knowing which of the many significations held by the trigram it changes into are relevant.

The best rule of thumb is (as in the example just given with Ch'ien): the containing signification—that is, the signification that should be in the foreground of our interpretation —should be one of those assigned the trigram *thrown*. We look to the trigram it is about to change into for further qualification of the situation or statement made by the first trigram. Therefore, if the thrown trigram is Ch'ien changing into Tui, the statement made by the changing Ch'ien trigram would not be the same as that arrived at if the reverse occurred—if the thrown hexagram were Tui, changing into Ch'ien. In the latter case the containing or important signification would be one of the many assigned Tui, those of Ch'ien then being secondary.

Further attributes of Ch'ien are a wheel, fellowship, firmness, strength, power or energy, time, motion, creative activity, and formlessness.

With the significations of the trigrams now in hand the reader can easily see that sometimes another picture that better explains the situation is contained in a hexagram. One such instance is found in Hexagram 28, Preponderance of the Great, where we are told the picture is of a beam with weak ends:

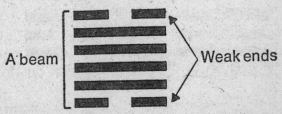

Hexagram #28—Preponderance of the Great

It is a difficult image to work with because we have been

told that the yang principle is light and without form. Here we have four yang lines with weight, a seeming contradiction. The trigram significations yield a much better image: that of a frozen lake whose edges are melting.

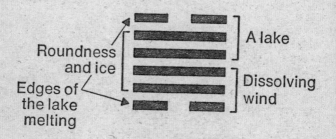

The upper trigram, Tui, is a lake; the upper and lower nuclear trigrams, Ch'ien in both cases, have as their significations ice and roundness; the lower primary trigram, Sun, is the wind that dissolves winter's ice. The image most definitely presents us with an instance where beginning and end, the edges of the lake, are weak.

In the emblems we saw ways of action, ways in which man may actively participate in the unending interplay of the opposites. In the trigrams the dynamics of change are revealed. Man may influence the ways of change but he may not alter the sequence within which change occurs, no more than he may alter the sequence of the sixty-four hexagrams. Here he is faced with the responsibility of aligning himself with the movement and operations of the spirit Tao. Only in that way can he survive the conflict of the opposites. He does this by making of the opposites complementary forces. Instead of causing them to come together in conflict, he allows them to approach one another in love. Their meeting then becomes one of creative union and birth rather than strife and conquest.

PART II

"That man who, giving up the purity by internal awareness, revels in external purity, that fool, O right-vowed sage! grasps a clod of earth, leaving off gold."

Dars'anopanisad, I:20–23

In the foregoing section we touched upon aspects of the trigrams pertinent to hexagram interpretation. In this section we will investigate aspects of the trigrams, as well as of the *Book of Changes* in general, little discussed by Westerners. Much that has already been mentioned will of necessity be reiterated in order to bring this section's topic—alchemy—into clearer focus.

This section will deal with components superimposed on the book's original structure. That the alchemical values imposed on it were later considerations may cause the reader to overlook their significance. The fact of the matter is that every aspect of the book lends itself to such alchemical interpretation, causing one to feel that the book is not yet complete, nor will it ever be as long as the underbelly of consciousness remains hidden. This is not to say the book's structure has still to undergo change, but that its meaning and message, as inexhaustible and infinite as the Tao it contains, will in time yield further appendices.

I

The divination of the future is essentially an inquiry into the personality of the individual. Our future is determined by our knowledge of ourselves, for through such knowledge we know the possibilities inherent in all alternatives presented to us in any situation. For this reason the *I Ching* is of great value to us. It cares little about the cruder aspects of divination. Its statement is a simple one: If the individual is truly in communion with that dimension of his personality which lends substance to life, he need neither know nor fear the future. All of his actions will be in accord with the time.

As discussed earlier, the *I Ching* as it exists today is a compendium of attempts by several generations of Chinese sages to discover the structure of the universe and its meaning for society and man. In it we find fragments of omentexts and divinatory techniques, numerology, astrology, natural science, history, philosophy, and religion. For this reason the book has with justification been called a "universal concept Repository." If it were not for the constant revision and commentary it has experienced in the hands of learned men, it would be little more than an encyclopedia of the sciences and the occult—at best, a fortune-telling device. What saved it from becoming only that was the foundation upon which it was constructed: the theory of the opposites.

Simply stated, the theory maintains that everything that exists in the universe has been generated out of one principle or field of unity. The framers of the *I Ching* were cognizant of the field as one containing immediate or a priori knowledge and sought to delineate it within the framework of a philosophical system which states that there is an equivalency of meaning between the macrocosm and microcosm. This made of the sixty-four hexagrams composing the book, pictorial representations of all possible archetypal events in the world. The *I Ching* tells us: "The changes have no consciousness or action; they are quiescent, nor do they move. If stimulated, they penetrate all situations under heaven." Which is to say that the sixty-four modes of spirit representing all experience in the world are the inherent possibilities of human action. They are archetypal in nature and may be given Jung's definition of the archetype in that they too are:

> based on a principle of form that has always been inherent in the psyche; they are inherited only in the sense that the structure of the psyche embodies a universally human heritage and bears within it the faculty of manifesting itself in definite and specific forms . . . they are channels, predispositions into which the water of life has dug deep. [Jolanda Jacobi, *Complex/Archetype/Symbol*, Bollingen Press]

In time this principle became identified with the human mind or, at least, with some plane of consciousness contained within the mind.

The concept of this principle or field of unity and its archetypal components is an old one. It is found in the Sanskrit *Lankavatra Scripture:*

> Universal mind transcends all individuation and limits . . . it is thoroughly pure in its essential nature, subsisting unchanged and free from faults of impermanence, undisturbed by egoism, unruffled by distinctions, desires and aversions . . .

> It is like a great ocean, its surface ruffled by waves and surges but its depths remaining forever unmoved. In itself it is devoid of personality and all that belongs to it, but by reason of defilement upon its face it is like an actor and plays a variety of parts, among which a mutual functioning takes place and the mind-system arises. The principle of intellection becomes divided and mind, the functions of mind, take on individuation . . . the seven fold gradation of mind appears . . . Universal mind is the storage and clearing house of all the accumulated products of mentation and action since beginningless time.

Not until the twentieth century, however, was the existence of this field substantiated and redefined:

> The original structural components of the psyche are of no less surprising a uniformity than are those of the visible body. The archetypes are, so to speak, organs of the prerational psyche. They are eternally inherited forms and ideas which have at first no specific content. Their specific content only appears in the course of the individual's life, when personal experience is taken up in precisely these forms . . . I must content myself with the hypothesis of an omnipresent, but undifferentiated, psychic structure which is inherited and which necessarily gives a certain form and direction to all experience. For, just as the organs of the body are not mere lumps of indifferent, passive matter, but are dynamic functional

complexes which assert themselves with imperious urgency, so also the archetypes, as organs of the psyche, are dynamic instinctual complexes which determine psychic life to an extraordinary degree. That is why I call them dominants of the unconscious. The layer of the unconscious psyche which is made up of these universal dynamic forms I have termed the collective unconscious. [C. G. Jung, Foreword to *The Tibetan Book of the Dead*, Evans Wentz, Oxford University Press]

The Tao of Chinese philosophy in every particular corresponds with this definition of the collective unconscious, or objective psyche.

But how, one might ask, does the mere casting of coins or stalks allow us to read the information of this dimension? Again, I must turn to Jung's observations for a possible explanation.

Jung, in his *Synchroncity: An Acausal Connecting Principle*, points out that the philosophical concept underlying the empirically based research of Occidental science is that of causality, which presupposes a unified field of time and space within which only it may be operative. The dynamic principle active in causality is defined as energy because "causality presupposes the existence of space and time insofar as all observations are ultimately based upon bodies in motion" ("The Structure and Dynamics of the Psyche"). Energy, as a measurable quality, is subject to the laws of time and space as we now know them.

Jung then points out that the experiments of J. B. Rhine at the Parapsychological Laboratories of Duke University indicate that the statistically proven cases of acausality exceeding the laws of probability were in no way effected by the time-space continuum and concludes that, contrary to popular belief, no transmission of energy took place. That is, if you, seated in a room a thousand miles away from me, correctly "receive" a picture transmitted by my concentrating on that picture in an attempt to relay it to you, we must assume that an actual transmission of wave or energy pulses has not transpired because neither time nor distance in any way effected "reception." If an actual transmission in the causal sense had occurred, if energy of any type had been beamed through the air toward you, it would have been measurable and the incident recorded as one residing within the realm of causality.

How, then, are correct guesses made in such tests? Inasmuch as the information received was not the result of exterior phenomena, Jung reasoned that the information was "a product of pure imagination, of 'chance' ideas which reveal the structure of that which produces them, namely, the unconscious." [*Collected Works of C. G. Jung,* Bollingen Press]

The problem parapsychological research is confronted with lies in the fact that the field is not always accessible. The phenomena the researchers attempt to measure is too dependent on the personalities tested. Recent studies in shamanistic techniques indicate that it is possible for certain types of individuals to have access to this sphere of information. We might, therefore, assume that the individual or individuals responsible for the creation of the *I Ching* received their intuitive knowledge of the archetypal structure of the field by such shamanistic techniques. What this means, in essence, is that the *I Ching* presents us with a statement about the structural qualities of the human psyche, the objective psyche in particular. The Oriental knew this objective psyche as Tao and understood it to be spirit, active and animating.

This spirit and its operations gain considerable prominence in later Chinese thought, becoming the focal point of many important commentaries on the *I Ching*. What startles one about these commentaries is that they are alchemical treatises that treat the book as an alchemical manual.

Because alchemy in this century has finally come to be understood as that spontaneous product of the unconscious that best outlines the process of personality development and transformation, the value of the *I Ching*'s employment as an alchemical text is for the first time discernible. Such alchemical treatment of the book actually enhances its message. Its lineaments may now transcend all barriers of language.

The *I Ching* might be likened to an alchemist's laboratory in that its "vessels" and "substances" might also be employed in the attempt to accelerate the process of psychological or spiritual transformation. I do not here attempt to foist a literary affectation on the reader. In an alchemical commentary on the *I Ching* of the first century A.D., we are told just that certain hexagrams of the book are understood as vessels, certain others as substances, and others as directives as to the proper time transformations should be undertaken.

II

The innumerable paradoxes and contradictions presented by the best of the alchemists at first suggest attempts to secretly transmit information of an extremely valuable nature to an elite community. This is in part true, for the alchemists did set forth the dynamics of an internal and psychic process by which the spiritual side of man could be awakened, transformed, and entered into eternity. The alchemist therefore believed in the importance of keeping the methods secret for much the same reason that prompted the Chinese sage to say that if the wrong man used the right methods, the right methods worked in the wrong way. To those whom he felt worthy of such consideration, the alchemist set forth what he believed to be sufficient leads; for the others, those who foolishly strove to make real gold, he continually furnished warnings to the effect that what was spoken of was not the common gold, not the common silver, not the common mercury, and that any interpretations based on such beliefs were those of fools and hypocrites of the highest order, bound to the grossness of their desires. But in the long run the obscurity of alchemical texts must be explained by the fact that the nature of the alchemist's experience overran that perimeter of sensibility one comfortably expects to find encompassing language. Theirs was a dialogue forced upon them, composed of an archetypal grammar generally known only to poets.

The alchemists held that gold had its origin in base metals and that, if such metals were allowed to remain within the earth for hundreds or thousands of years, they would reach the stage of perfection exemplified by gold. The alchemist, therefore, by working on metals, sought to aid nature by accelerating the process. But it must be kept in mind that the alchemist time and again tells us in his writings that what he seeks is not the base metal gold, but something of a subtler nature, something one cannot hold in one's hand. To know what it was he sought, we must first investigate what he believed the nature of matter was.

Simply put, matter, and specifically metal, contained an animating principle that outwardly transformed the thing containing it. It was this principle, this spirit, that the alchemists sought to aid, for they believed it to be a portion of the active principle that had become ensnared in matter at the moment of creation. For this reason one often finds Occidental alchemists alluding to the happenings of Genesis when they discuss the stages and operations of their work. In aiding this spirit in its effort of transformation, the alchemists understood the Garden of Eden to be a limited field. The fruit of consciousness having been tasted, perfection as innocence came to a close.

The serpent, symbol par excellence of transformation, revealed to incipient consciousness—the consciousness capable of "naming animals," that is, capable of making qualitative distinctions—that the greatest sin one endowed with humanity could commit was the unwillingness to escape from the innocence of ignorance. Time and again we are presented with the figure of the exiled Adam, body composed of impure elements, as one who must be rid of his impurities. The elements of innocence found in the child become impurities in the grown man, who, having passed beyond the protective circle of childhood, must fend for himself and cope with the harsh and arid reality surrounding him.

The development and transformation of those components that define the personality as human and individual might be likened to the process the alchemist believed metals underwent in the earth. What the alchemist realized was that the wholeness and completion understood to be but an adjunct of old age could and should be realized earlier in life. That is, what we too often recognize as the limit of ourselves is but the particular of a developmental stage and that the common human failing is to accept the transitional as the pattern for a lifetime. The alchemists intuitively understood what twentieth-century psychology is beginning to substantiate: What is truly personal, what is truly individual in the personality, truly contained in "earth," is subject to change whether or not the personality participates in the event. But, as the *I Ching* tells us, all change is performed before a backdrop of permanency within which the ambiguities of good and evil are relative. This is what is meant by the *I Ching*'s statement that change is that which does not change. That which causes change, is changed, and is in itself unchangeable, is Tao.

This Tao, or spirit, has always been regarded as a principle residing in man as well as matter. Always, we find the term employed wherever attempts were made to explain, on the one hand, the motivating principle in animate matter, and on the other, the discerning quality of mind that distinguishes man from animal. The alchemist in both Occident and Orient understood this and therefore sought to bring man to that state comparable to the supreme value assigned gold. The problem they were faced with was age-old: If, at the beginning of time, a substance existed from which all inanimate matter originally sprang, the original man, the pure and unsullied state of being, still existed in man. They called this unknown factor *prima materia,* prime matter.

Reading the alchemists, one is immediately struck with the thousands of definitions and sources of *prima materia.* It becomes immediately apparent that each had his own understanding as to the nature of this material, and that each respected, no matter how contradictory to his own definition it was, the findings of his peers. The implication is one that leads us to accept the premise put forth by certain twentieth-century investigators that *prima materia* was not a substance to the alchemists but a symbol. That the substance to be transformed was not material but spiritual, metaphysical, or psychological is borne out by several authors. If we read in the writings of one alchemist that *prima materia* is excrement and then find in the writings of another that it is not only that but peacock flesh as well, then we are obviously faced with a situation where the objects referred to are but signs pointing to an inexpressible meaning or understanding that each has found in the object he speaks of. The effect varies, but the cause is one.

As one alchemist plainly put it: "This substance is extracted from you, and you are its mineral; in you they find it, and, that I may speak more plainly, from you they take it." Dorn, the disciple of Paracelsus, goes a bit further: "There is in natural things a certain truth which cannot be seen with the outward eye, but is perceived by the mind alone . . . In this lies the whole art of freeing the spirit from its fetters." Here, clearly, *prima materia* is equated with meaning, for that which cannot be perceived by the senses is not of this world but of another, invisible, defined by Dorn as mind. To know the truth of something is to know its meaning, its prime cause. The *prima materia* of the alchemists was, simply put, meaning.

Here one must accept Jung's valuable contention that because the concept of *prima materia* was a carrier for the autonomous psychic content of the alchemist, it was impossible for a specific substance to exist in which all the qualities assigned prime matter could be found. Because, in essence, the substance referred to and sought after had a metaphysical rather than an empirical reality, the *materia* was formed or brought into focus by the *personality* of the alchemist. The object unconsciously selected for the projection of autonomous content held a specific value into which the investment of libido or psychic energy was deposited. For that reason alone every alchemist had his own *prima materia*. Herein lies the secret: Wherever a disproportionate investment of energy is found, there, if one digs deep enough, is *prima materia*. Because the philosopher's stone, the end product of the alchemist's labor, and *prima materia* are equated in their writings, this is of great import. Since the stone is "all things" and the *prima materia* a small and often rejected thing, we find ourselves with Blake's "world in a grain of sand": the reduction, and therefore retrieval, of energy, any form of energy from any object whether empirically or metaphysically perceived, has as its source a common and limited ground, a ground in which everything is relative. What this means is that to find the meaning of any one event or idea is to find *prima materia*, a successful conclusion.

If one approaches the *I Ching* with a problem and accepts the hexagram received as a solution that must first be deciphered before it can be integrated with his life, then one is working with *prima materia*. The decipherment of the hexagram gives meaning to the situation; where confusion and conflict reigned there is suddenly understanding. The first function the *I Ching*'s hexagrams perform is the temporary alleviation of the tension present in any given situation. By doing this the individual is afforded the opportunity of viewing his situation objectively, in a clearer light, and determining which of many alternatives is the proper course of action.

It would be a great error to assume all of life to be little more than a coming and a going. It is a dynamic process wherein one may discover and unfold the whole of history that has preceded one, thereby discovering one's place in the order, and one's meaning. For it is meaning that absolves, eradicates all contradiction, meaning that reveals chaos and misunderstanding as being little more than the ignorance of a moment, whether the moment be measured by an hour or a lifetime, the ignorance, truly, that lash us toward the desire of knowledge. Only one who has tasted consciousness may suffer this.

The alchemist is one who through a conscientious and conscious consideration of himself attempts to reconcile the opposing tendencies in himself.

III

Too often we find moral and ethical traditions fixed frameworks within which the individual must discover his proper slot and remain. That individualism which marks man as unique among creatures must be sacrificed in the name of tradition. True, such systems are often a necessary adjunct to the development of consciousness, which by definition demands that limitations be set for the unconscious and instinctual portion of himself that man shares with the lower orders. Only a spiritual or social revolution can break such bonds, and periodically broken they must be if the active and positive spirit of evolution is not to stagnate.

Without exception, such moments in history find the individual at a loss for any set of guiding principles. Because any interruption in the process of evolution, whether of the race or of the personality, ultimately expresses itself as conflict, the individual must resolve the tension of the moment so that he might at least survive the event. Because self-consciousness offers the possibility—not necessarily the promise—of extension and amplification, it must be viewed as an evolutionary trust granted man. To it, and therefore to himself, he must be responsible. To fulfill this responsibility he must not only be receptive to the knowledge and creative manipulation of external events, but must seek an awareness and acceptance of his own capabilities in any given situation. Only by doing so can he maintain his individuality.

Here then is the relevance of the *I Ching:* It attempts to serve man by showing him the way to the unity hidden within. At most, it asks that he recognize the interplay of the opposites as the cause of all causes, incipient forces molding the *materia* of circumstances. In short, the book is an instrument of transformation that attempts to align the individual with the original unity, the Tao, thereby making his life a perpetual unfolding and reintegration with the forces that at every moment effect him.

Even the most careless consideration of one's nature will reveal that it is bounded by a permanency and consistency of being that irrefutably represents itself as "me," while at the same time revealing a flux, a progressive movement backward and forward in time, whereby one is caused to be occasionally aware of the propensity toward change residing within oneself. Both states, that of permanency and flux, are the attributes of Tao as found in the *I Ching*. The book is as unified a field as the Tao it represents because that which perseveres, perseveres because it is imbued with spirit. Captured within its form is meaning of an order beyond the exhaustible or reductible.

The field of Tao, of immediate knowledge, is the mandala of earlier heaven. This, in conjunction with the equally important Lo Shu, outlines several processes of becoming. The one we will now concern ourselves with is the creation and birth of an idea. In discussing these two diagrams as being representative of ideational processes, reference will be made to C. G. Jung's theory of the four complexes. Although my analysis of the diagrams leans heavily on this theory, I by no means attempt to present myself as an interpreter of so complex a thesis. At most, I borrow the terminology—apologizing for any disservice I might perform in presenting Jung's ideas within so conjectural a viewpoint.

PART III

In Chapter II of the appendix called "Discussion of the Trigrams (Shuo Kua)," we find the following:

Direction is determined by heaven and earth. In union are the forces of mountain and lake. Aroused by one another are thunder and wind. Water and fire do not fight with one another. In this way the eight trigrams come together and mingle.

This refers us to the diagram discussed in passing earlier, the sequence of early heaven or the primal arrangement where the opposites are paired off with one another:

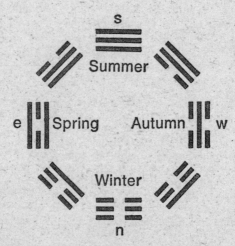

The diagram relates the trigrams to seasonal periods as well as compass points. Each trigram not only reigns over a season but is symbolic of that season. The trigram K'un, exemplar of darkness and containment, also stands for winter. The east, place of the sun's daily birth, has as its symbol the trigram Li, which stands for the sun. The balancing of the opposites here indicates an ideal condition, the moment when both time and space are in accord with one another; the moment when, instead of tension resulting from the meeting of contraries, there exists instead their complementary and loving union.

Because this diagram speaks of the harmony of the universe and its powers, the world as demarcated by the four compass points, and the human mind as a mandala depicting the desired course of psychic energy, it may be thought of as a mystery diagram, which, if contemplated, will in time reveal everything. At least, so the ancient Chinese thought. To understand this diagram as a microcosmic blueprint is to have the opportunity of aligning oneself with the universal harmony, the Tao. For one to be in Tao, as the Orientals say, it is necessary for one to understand the movement of the valley spirit not only throughout the universe, but within oneself as well. This is the function and gift of the *Book of Changes*. Through it we may learn how to be in Tao every moment of our lives.

The appendix goes on to tell us that if one

. . . counts what is going into the past, he must first know of the forward movement; to know what is yet to come, he must know of the backward movement . . .

This mention of forward- and backward-moving lines cannot be understood without the material presented in the following paragraph:

Movement is brought about by thunder, dispersion by wind, moisture by rain, warmth by the sun, the time of standstill by Keeping Still, pleasure by the Joyous, ruler or kingship by the Creative, shelter by the Receptive.

Here we discover that the forward-moving line is that created by the entry of the first four trigrams' powers in the universe:

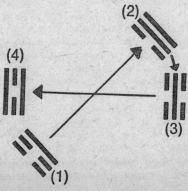

The backward-moving line is composed of Kên, Tui, Ch'ien, and K'un and is called backward-moving because of the sudden shift from Li in the east to Kên in the northwest:

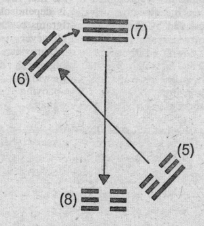

The first four trigrams, which comprise the forward-moving line, are referred to as effects or forces that are eternally operative; that is, they represent forces operating in the universe beyond the earthly plane. The last four trigrams, those comprising the backward-moving line, speak of conditions that take place on earth during the course of a year. The first four are cause; the last four, effect. The *Book of Changes* tells us that to know what is becoming part of the past, that is, what is becoming fixed in history, what is substantially pertinent and therefore real, it is necessary to know the movement of the forward-moving line made up of the first four trigrams. It is what the present opens out on that defines which of all coordinates or seeming realities existing but a moment ago were real. The backward-moving line, composed of the last four trigrams, prepares the future through contraction. Contraction may be explained as follows: If the time of puberty is understood as that time when the human organism is finally complete, the years preceding puberty may be thought of as forward-moving because it is the purpose of nature to strive toward completion. The years after puberty or maturation are the years following completion. This forward-moving line from biological completion to death is a contraction for it leads the organism back to its beginnings.

What this diagram essentially reveals is the manner in which cosmic time—represented by the first four trigrams—gives birth to, is supportive of, and is dependent on earthly time—represented by the last four trigrams revealing the sequence of events as found in nature. However, it is when this diagram is viewed as the psychic structure discussed earlier —the mandala—that its most interesting aspects are revealed. To discuss this aspect of the diagram it will first be necessary to look to another diagram accompanying the *Book of Changes*—the Ho T'u, or Yellow River map.

The Ho T'u

The Ho T'u symbolically presents the manner in which an idea comes into being. Diagrammed simply, it looks like this:

```
                        Fire
                        (2)
Wood (3)                                    (4) Metal
                        (1)
                        Water
```

The following presentation grows out of an objective and careful consideration of the material by one researcher. It is up to the reader to modify or amplify, to determine the worth of another's consideration of so complex a matter as the book we here attempt to discuss.

As mentioned in an earlier chapter, the elements were anciently understood to represent different functions or components of the personality. Jung's formulation of the four functions, I believe, is the scientific presentation of these components. Instead of fire, earth, air, and water we find thinking, feeling, intuition, and sensation. In his view these four functions are ways of perceiving or being present to the world. One of the four becomes uppermost in the individual in early childhood and serves him as a primary function; that is, he views and experiences the world through the qualities of the predominating function. However, the idea is to make at least three of the four functions available to the individual. (I refer the reader to Jung's *Psychological Types* for further information and elucidation.) The important thing to point out for our purposes is that in Jung's model of the four functions, the functions are dynamic—any one of the four may come to predominate. In our discussion, we will speak of the four as having a fixed and sequential nature. The Yellow River map shows the order and sequence of their appearance and operation: Water is the first element, fire the second, wood the third, and metal the fourth. To these elements correspond, respectively, the four functions of intuition, sensation, feeling, and thinking.

Sensation
(fire)

Feeling   Thinking
(wood)   (metal)

(water)
Intuition

Water

The first element is water, symbolic of the function of intuition. An idea in its original state is undifferentiated; those qualities that would distinguish it from other older and realized contents of the mind have not yet been perceived and delineated. Its components form an undifferentiated clump or cluster of potential energy. The idea is first encountered as a whole and is apprehended suddenly; it is not the result of deductive analysis and reasoning. Deductive reasoning most often precedes an idea's appearance, but the idea itself first emerges as an undifferentiated whole, seemingly indivisible. That an idea is a cluster of potential energy may be shown by the excitement that usually accompanies it. The excitement is at first unbridled; in time it becomes the energy by which the further ramifications of the idea are pursued.

Here we see the idea in its original state: as formless and uncontained as the ocean. The idea has not yet been received; it has only been felt, intuited. A presence has been recorded, and little more.

Fire

The original unity of the idea and the intuitive recognition of it, here give place to its conscious recognition and perception. The light that fire gives off, the "knowledge" that fire reveals, is here assigned to the second state of ideation: perception. This process of original unity, followed by perception, is a familiar motif in mythology.

In the tantric text, *Kama-Kala-Vilasa*, we are told that Shiva, the active and masculine principle in the universe, stood contemplating himself at the beginning of time. Knowledge of himself—self-knowledge—did not occur, however, until Shakti, the feminine and devoted principle of the universe residing in him, out of pure love separated herself from him so that she could stand as mirror in which his radiance might be reflected for his eyes to see. Seeing himself he said, "I Am," and his unity was realized.

It is in this stage that the wholeness of the idea is perceived; here that the idea becomes a distinct entity worthy of attention. It has been separated out by perception, the light of awareness represented here by fire. The first stage was apprehension; the second, perception. Up to this point no effort of will has been exercised. The intuition was a spontaneous occurrence; the perception, a mechanical, automatic operation. It is only in the last two stages that a conscious participation in the event occurs.

Wood

In fire and water we found two opposite movements representative of yin and yang—one up and one down; the first an extraverted and outward-flowing movement, the second, an inward and downward, contemplative movement. The yin-and-yang pulse is here contained in one element—wood—and takes on a plus and minus value of like and dislike. It can easily be seen how a tree symbolically contains these oppositional qualities within it. On the one hand we find the upward-moving tendency of a tree expressed by its branches and trunk; on the other, a downward-moving tendency, in the roots. The energy originally employed in the formation and maintenance of the contemplative and extraverted attitudes here becomes that which gives birth to feeling, the third movement in our diagram. The thing perceived is here the subject of a value judgment: of liking or disliking. Here the personality for the first time consciously participates in the event. The value of the idea is considered within the context of the situation it appears to refer to.

Metal

This last element is an apt representative of that aspect of mind that discriminates, cuts, and divides reality as a metal knife would. It stands for that aspect of mind that distinguishes gradations finer than perceived through the process of valuation. This element corresponds to the thinking function, which distinguishes "this" from "that."

Now to return to the sequence of earlier heaven. Viewed as a mandala depicting an operation of mind, the first four movements of the diagram—those of thunder, wind, sun, and moon—speak of the birth of the idea beyond the sphere of the personal human mind, within the sphere of the objective psyche. These first four movements refer us to an experience that transcends consciousness by its cosmic nature; the last four, to that which takes place within the realm of consciousness. The moment between the first four movements and the last four movements is symbolically presented to us in the Yellow River map. What the diagram states is that the spirit Tao first expresses itself as sound, thunder—a rumbling in the maw of eternity. This corresponds to the many creation myths in which we are told that the first act of creation is sound—or, as the New Testament tells us, "In the beginning was the Word."

Tantric philosophy relates that the essence of the universe is contained in a sacred syllable, a sound. According to the great mystic Jacob Behmen, the beginning is announced by a flash of fire, accompanied by the word *Mercurius*. This first moment of creation is represented by the trigram Chên, thunder. The Chinese assign this trigram to the time of spring, when all things awake from their winter slumber. The activation of the male principle that has been slumbering throughout the cold season is accompanied by thunder and movement. As early as the third century B.C. we find, in the *Li*

Ki, or *Book of Rites,* that spring is the time when "thunder speaks and lightning is seen." The book goes on to tell us that three days before the vernal equinox a bell with a wooden tongue was sounded as warning against improper behavior.

The second aspect of spirit, and its most popular form in religion and mythology, is wind, here represented by the trigram Sun. In the Old Testament we are told that after the first sound, the Word, the spirit of God moved upon the face of the waters. In the creation myth presented us in the primal arrangement this wind serves to break up the rigid yin principle, the ice formed in winter. Wind here performs the act of separation in much the same way that the Old Testament spirit divided "the waters which were under the firmament from the waters which were above the firmament." But the most important act of division performed by this spirit wind is revealed in the following two trigrams of K'an and Li.

The ice dispersed by the wind trigram gives birth to the trigram for water, K'an, which also represents the moon; this in turn yields the trigram Li, fire and the sun. Again, this follows the pattern of many creation myths, including that found in the Old Testament. There, after the spirit wind has moved upon the face of the waters, the Creator divides light from darkness. In the Chinese creation myth, the sun and the moon, symbolic of light and darkness, become separated out by the action of the wind.

It is understood that, in our diagram, once the sun and moon have come into being, the moisture of the moon and the heat of the sun are directed toward the diagram's center where the seed resides. It will be remembered that yang and yin, in the diagram of the supreme ultimate outlining their separation out of T'ai Chi, were likened to the sun and moon respectively, and only after their separation out of the original unity did the elements come into being. The Yellow River map outlines the birth of the elements. It is for this reason that it is thought of as coming into existence or residing in that moment between the first four movements and the last four movements of the map of the primal heaven. The seed residing at the center of this map is the Yellow River map, or rather the operations of the elements. The separation and marriage of the sun and the moon, which symbolically represent the conscious and the unconscious, and their eventual cooperation in the creation and shaping of an idea is the major theme of both the sequence of earlier heaven (primal arrangement) and the Yellow River map. As we shall see when we discuss the diagram known as the Lo Shu, or writing from the River Lo, this moment is prerequisite for spiritual fulfillment and completion for the commentators on the *I Ching*. In these diagrams is hidden a process and method of transformation of significant proportion. It is the meaning behind the metaphysical statement that the elements do not come into being before the formation of the yin-yang pulse.

The last four movements of the primal arrangement, those performed by the trigrams of Keeping Still, the Gentle, Heaven, and Earth speak of the conscious and controlled manipulation of the idea and its fruit.

The time of Keeping Still (Kên) refers us to the moment when the idea is taken in hand and brought to active fruition anticipating application. This trigram has as one of its major significations that of the mountain, which is composed of stone and earth gathered at one fixed point. The time therefore speaks of a gathering together of all elements necessary to support and maintain the idea.

The next trigram, Tui, the Gentle or lake, represents the season of harvest, the time of the final gathering. Here selection is made, and what is selected is given form. The trigram also stands for the mouth, or communication. The thing or idea is worked on and given a form that can be transmitted —it becomes a book, a poem, or a working plan.

The sign of the Creative (Ch'ien) stands for the head and the intellectual application of the results of all that has gone before. The trigram K'un, the earth and Receptive, marks the end of the movement when all the energy or spirit employed returns to its source.

The Lo Shu

The Lo Shu, or writing from the River Lo, appended to the *I Ching*, is an inconspicuous diagram of seemingly little import. However, as we shall see, it is an alchemical talisman. The important thing to bring out immediately is that it is a magic square of 15:

```
4 9 2
3 5 7
8 1 6
```

Any three numbers on a straight line total 15. We have been
told time and again by neo-Confucians and Taoists that the
number of Tao is 15. Of the many ways one can think of to
answer the question why the creators of the *Book of Changes*
chose the numbers 6, 7, 8, and 9 to signify yin and yang in
their static and dynamic aspects, this way appears to yield the
most apparent answer: a changing yin (6) and a changing
yang (9), as well as an unchanging yin (8) and an unchanging yang (7), when added together yield 15—Tao.

Let us see if we can find the origin of this magic square in
Chinese culture. Because it is a common talisman found in
the occult literature of other countries, one is tempted to dis-
miss it as being an importation appended to the *Book of
Changes* as an afterthought. To fully comprehend the significance of its appearance in the *I Ching*, we will review its appearance earlier in the history of Chinese culture.

During the Chou dynasty (403–221 B.C.) there existed a
square temple of nine rooms called the Ming T'ang, or Hall

9th month	10th month	11th month	12th month	1st month
8th month		Season of the Center		2nd month
7th month	6th month	5th month	4th month	3rd month

of Light, where the emperor performed all the religious and ceremonial functions necessary for the maintenance of the kingdom.

On the first day of each month the emperor, dressed in robes symbolic of the season, performed with the aid of other court dignitaries the sacrifices and rituals necessary to insure that the season before them was entered properly. This temple was a model of the path through which the heavenly powers of the universe moved. The emperor, or son of heaven, by entering the rooms and regulating the powers of earth with those of heaven, made these rooms sacred. The rituals he performed were quite detailed and can be found in the ancient Chinese document, the *Li Chi*, in the Chapter on "Proceedings of Government in the Different Months". What is important for our discussion is the fact that the rooms were numbered after the fashion of a magic square. We do not know whether this was done intentionally. What is important is that later alchemists noted the correspondence and, knowing that the rooms of the Hall of Light were models of the monthly and universal powers, assigned this mathematical structure to the trigrams meant to imply that the operator who held and used such a talisman would in his own right be a son of heaven.

The full significance that the magic square and the trigrams came to hold for the alchemists is revealed in a treatise of the second century A.D., known as the *Ts'an T'ung Ch'i*. In this work, all alchemical operations are spoken of as dependent on the knowledge of the meaning of the trigrams and hexagrams of the *Book of Changes*. In the very first chapter reference is made to the diagram of early heaven; and the four most important trigrams, Ch'ien (heaven), K'un (earth), K'an (moon), and Li (sun) are likened to the four walls of a city, the latter two trigrams' operations representing a wheelhub which, while spinning the wheel, holds the axle in place. In other words, what holds the diagram of early heaven together is the operation of the sun and moon.

The objective of the alchemical operations described in the text is the creation of a subtle body, an homunculus. It is on the fifteenth day of the moon, when it is full, that the Ch'ien body is formed. Here, clearly, the number 15 stands for perfection and completion. The number represents gold, the philosopher's stone, the self. By superimposing the diagram of early heaven on the magic square of 15, the alchemists revealed the operations of the trigrams to be not only those of change, but of transformation and transmutation as well. When we read in Chapter 16 of the *Ts'an T'ung Ch'i* that one must insure the well-being of his inner self by directing all attention inward, and by so doing arrive at a state of perfect peace during which time the prime substance contained within him will illuminate the interior of his being, we must admit that the text refers us to a process of spiritual transformation.

Chapter 5

In this final chapter we will analyze a hexagram from start to finish. The analysis is of an answer received during a recent seminar of mine in New York City. The question was, "What meaning have you, the *Book of Changes,* for the Occidental?" One line was thrown once a week for a period of six weeks, and Hexagram 16, Enthusiasm, with the third line moving, was received in answer to this question.

The first line received was an 8:

 (8)

There is little this one line can tell us except to indicate that the underlying attitude or support will have had as its parent the feminine or yin principle; that is, we can expect to be confronted with the depiction of a situation that will demand adherence to the quiescent and receptive temper of the spirit Tao.

The second line thrown was another 8:

 (8)
(8)

The emblem is that of water. The hexagram will not only have as its foundation the feminine principle, but that specifically quiescent and receptive state of contemplation. Water is that which moves downward, and is therefore symbolic of introspection.

The third line was a 6, a moving line:

 (6)
(8)
(8)

The trigram before us is K'un, the earth. It is the trigram

of the mother, that which nourishes. Because this trigram is in the lower part of the hexagram, it defines the nature of the subjective aspect of the hexagram. Again, the emphasis is on the feminine mode of action, or nonaction.

The fourth line received was a 7:

Here it must be kept in mind that the question had to do with a collective body of individuals. An attribute of K'un, the lower primary trigram, that seems to coincide with this aspect of the question, is a group of people or a nation. However, any nation may be referred to here. The attribute that identifies the nation—and therefore tells us that at least up to this point the lines are specifically addressing themselves to the question—does so without beating about the bush: K'un is also a vessel or a pot in which things, through the action of cooking, are broken down, transformed, and united. Therefore, the nation referred to is one that might be likened to a pot—a melting pot, in short. Because K'un also stands for the world, the nation is thought of as the melting pot of the world.

The upper nuclear trigram is Kên, the mountain, the symbol for keeping still. Both trigrams, K'un and Kên, press downward, halting outward movement. This cessation of movement is emphasized by the fact that the lower primary trigram also changes into Kên:

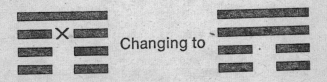

Changing to

At the same time, the trigram Kên further defines the situation by presenting us with the image of something large. Here we have the picture of a large nation that might be likened to a melting pot.

What is there about the earth or a nation that may be kept still? Because the earth is the element out of which all things are produced, the image is of a nation devoted to production, or outward manifestation. By changing into the trigram of keeping still, the lower nuclear trigram (also Kên) changes into Sun, the wind.

One of the attributes of this trigram is that of men close to profit and gain—men so much involved with profit and gain that they get a threefold return on their wares. Again, the image refers us to the country in question, a rich nation.

In the diagram of earlier heaven this trigram's function is the breaking up of winter's ice. It is therefore the trigram of work and toil. The *Book of Changes* tells us that the trigram also stands for height and length. Therefore, this trigram speaks of measurements, of blueprints and outlines, of carefully plotted methods aimed at reaching an objective. These significations taken together present us with the image of the toil involved in the measurement of things.

The trigram also speaks of advance and retreat, in much the same way that the wind advances and retreats. Why does something continually advance and retreat? Because it is indecisive. The necessity of measuring and plotting things this trigram speaks of grows out of indecisiveness. How has this indecisiveness come about? Note that the changing line is contained in the emblem for fire.

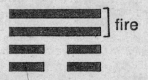

Fire speaks of that which is formless. In order to remain alive fire must leap from one form to another, feeding indiscriminately, advancing and withdrawing in much the same way the wind does. What is important to fire is that it keep alive. Nothing in its nature is fixed.

This is emphasized by yet another image. The trigram Sun stands for a boat; the emblem one might say Sun is on top of is water. The image is of a boat on the water—an image which in the *Book of Changes* is associated with the idea of crossing a great body of water. Looking up this combination of images in the *I Ching*, we discover Hexagram 59, Dispersion:

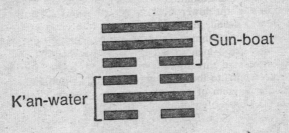

Hexagram 59 speaks of the dispersion and dissolving of divisive egotism. Here we might have reference to a quality of the fire emblem. Fire does not discriminate. Whatever it encounters it devours. It thinks of nothing but its own maintenance. The emblem may therefore also stand for the inflation often accompanying one who supposes no doors are closed to him.

The statement the trigram appears to make up to this point is that the condition of indecisiveness is a dangerous one and one which must be changed by a crossing of the great water.

You will notice that the original question directed itself to Occidental man in general; the lines here refer us to the United States in particular.

We have on the one hand learned that the images refer us to the idea of a large and productive nation and that that nation may be likened to a pot within which things are transformed. Where the lower trigram changes into Kên, the images are either speaking of a time when such outward productivity will come to an end, or suggesting that such activity be consciously brought to an end. The doubling of the trigram Kên reminds us of the hexagram called Keeping Still, Number 52. There we are told that the superior man does not let his thought go beyond the immediate situation. That this statement is significant in this context will be borne out as we now discuss the nuclear hexagrams contained in the lines before us.

The lower nuclear hexagram is made up of the lower primary trigram K'un and the upper nuclear trigram Kên, to yield Hexagram 23, Splitting Apart.

In accordance with the philosophy of change such times are within the natural order of things. This linear tension, or orderly progression of events, is known to us as the Sequence, each sequence note appended to a hexagram referring to the hexagram immediately preceding it. The time of a hexagram is the direct result of a linear progression in both time and space. The time outlined by a hexagram is a "natural" result of the Sequence. Before speaking of the Sequence, let us look at the time of Splitting Apart:

The hexagram shows the last line, which is male, active, and creative, about to be pushed out of the picture. The dark lines, the lines of the receptive and devoted force, mount upward and will soon be in complete control of the situation. The last line of the hexagram tells us that the yang force, which is on its way out, may be likened to a ripe fruit. On the surface, the time is a precarious one because the principle of consciousness must not only drop down, but by entering the earth must become temporarily extinguished. But the fruit contains the seeds of the future. The moment speaks of rebirth. You will notice that the hexagram immediately following is Return, in which the Sequence reads, "Objects cannot be destroyed forever. When what has been above has been fully split apart, it returns below."

The hexagram of Splitting Apart refers us to the idea that the time of devotion to principles contained within the earth, the individual personality, is imminent. The last line of intellectual and rational being is overthrown. The devotional and receptive properties of the feminine principle come to the fore and dictate the way of the time—devotion. The feminine soul is allowed positive expression because she receives the seeds of the future. That which returns to the earth suffers death only as a prerequisite for rebirth.

On the other hand, such splitting apart in actual day-to-day experience can be terrifying. For the Occidental, the last barrier and final defense of all he may call rational and logical is thereby threatened. The feminine principle, which we in the West would call irrational, refers us to the realm of experience where sequential or "meaningful" order cannot be discovered. Instead, the moment is permeated either by so-called chance occurrences or by spontaneous and seemingly uncontrollable effects in which all intellectual consideration is bypassed in favor of the immediate emotional response. The time resembles what is known as the time of loose ends, when the yang principle, the rational attitude toward life and the world, is falling to pieces.

To recapitulate: The lines received up to this point speak of a large and rich nation whose rational and extroverted attitude is drawing rapidly to a close. Why has this come about? Here we must refer to the Sequence: "When one has too much adorned oneself, success is exhausted." Simply put, the time of splitting apart has come about because of a concern with outward appearances, and, possibly, in this instance, because of a devotion to production with an eye to profit and gain, as brought out by the trigrams. You will recall that the receptive or yin quality must be activated and led by the creative or yang quality if it is to manifest itself in its devotional and complementary aspect. In the event the yin force is not properly attended to, it presents its dark and destructive face in its attempt to overpower and supplant the light.

Here a point must be made about the Sequence of events as depicted in the *I Ching*. Earlier, we made the statement that the Sequence is the result of a natural series of events. Here, however, the implication is that the time of splitting apart has come about because of some deficiency. If one views the hexagram as being only one of the many manifestations of one spirit, then he can easily understand that it is not important to the spirit how it manifests itself, but only that it does so within its own prescribed sequence. This time of splitting apart, therefore, may come about as the direct result of a positive condition or may be the result of a purely negative condition. It does not matter to the spirit Tao whether it appears as negative or positive to the world. The important thing is that it manifests itself. It is totally unaffected by moral considerations. Only we are affected by such considerations. That is why we can make the seemingly contradictory statement that the time of splitting apart is a natural event in the order of things, but that in this instance its appearance is the result of a negative attitude.

The time of splitting apart occurs when one has gone too far in adornment. Adornment has to do with façades, outward manifestations, the type of action the yang principle promotes. This comes about because the extroverted and outward-moving yang principle, has ignored the feminine, devoted, and introverted yin principle. Introverted and personalistic energies have been relegated to the social sphere. Unity has been sought at the collective level at the expense of individual unity. The extroverted and rationalistic activity of the Occident has been carried on at the expense of the contemplative and uncompetitive attitude that complements it.

Our analysis has led us to this further statement: A great nation stands before the time of splitting apart. The time has come about because of too one-sided an attitude. The active male principle has been too much in the fore. All has been movement. Now the time of introspection, contemplation, and devotion forces itself on us. Up to this point the *Book of Changes* has only outlined our condition. It has not yet offered any solution. But we might find a solution in the second nuclear hexagram.

The second hexagram is made up of the lower primary trigram K'un and the "changed" lower nuclear trigram Sun. The hexagram so produced is Number 20, Contemplation:

Our attention is drawn to this nuclear hexagram because it holds an image we have noticed before, that of a tree. In Splitting Apart the image was that of fruit on a tree branch; here it is that of a tree in the distance. Later, when we discuss yet another nuclear hexagram, Number 53, Gradual Development, we will find the image of the tree on a mountain. The reason we say these particular nuclear hexagrams are pertinent is that they have or share a particular piece of information in common, in this instance, a tree.

It is not enough to know we are in the process of splitting apart. One may easily discern that without knowing the solution. Hidden within such moments lies an answer. In Hexagram 23, Splitting Apart, we are witness to the moment when the fruit is ready to fall. It is a moment of great transition. The sequence for Hexagram 20 reads: "When things have become great, then one may contemplate them." And the image reads. "In ancient times the kings visited the regions of the world, contemplated the people they found, and then gave instruction." In China the emperor regulated the ways of the world so that his kingdom might be in accord with the way of heaven. He was the earthly equivalent of the divine ruler. During certain times of the year he journeyed to distant parts of his kingdom to discover the needs of his people. Here, the *Book of Changes* likens itself to a king who seeks to give us instruction. The commentary tells us that in such a way the king allows us to comprehend the divine way of heaven.

On the one hand the book tells us how understanding came to us; on the other, it tells us that in times of splitting apart one must contemplate the splitting apart. The hexagram of Contemplation refers us to the image of a tree on a mountain seen from a great distance. The great distance symbolizes objectivity—from a distance one can see more.

The fruit of splitting apart will mark the period of transition by falling. What does this mean? Contemplation speaks of the moment of sacrifice, that moment when everything has been prepared. Here, the fruit is about to fall. The moment has arrived, the fruit is complete, the seeds of the future are contained within it. The fruit may be thought of as sacrificing itself by falling to the ground and decaying so that the seeds of the future may be born. Splitting Apart, in this instance, is the hexagram of sacrifice. Surely such moments require contemplation. The active principle of the world is being forced to leave the field of action, to give itself up to the natural cycle of things.

The appended judgment also tells us that splitting apart means decay. What does decay mean? Again, we turn to the *I Ching* as a dictionary of symbols, and find Hexagram 18, Work on What Has Been Spoiled (Decay).

The Chinese character after which this hexagram is named pictures a sacrificial bowl containing food infested with worms. The moment of sacrifice has been prepared for but is so long in coming that the thing sacrificed has become the home of maggots. The hexagram of Splitting Apart tells us that the time is synonymous with the time of decay, and adds that for the future to be born it is first necessary that the fruit containing its seed fall and decay. Recall that in the lines we have received in answer to our question the trigram for bowl (K'un) appears. The nation spoken of is therefore likened to a bowl in which things are in a state of decay. In order to find out the specific nature of this decay it is imperative that we see how Hexagram 18, Decay, becomes the hexagram of Splitting Apart, Number 23. It is when the second and third lines of this hexagram are moving that this occurs:

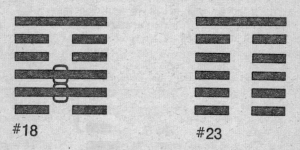

#18   #23

The text accompanying the second line of Hexagram 18 tells us that when a son deals with the troubles or decay that have been caused by the mother, he should not be too persevering and harsh in his action. What has caused the decay? The casual indifference of the feminine or yin principle.

The third line tells us that there will be little remorse in correcting or setting right what has come into decay because

of the father. What has been the father's (or yang principle's) fault? The male principle has been too active. Wilhelm's commentary goes on to explain that too much energy
is better than too little. The excess has grown out of the attitude expressed in the saying, "Where there's a will there's a
way." Since the turn of the seventeenth century the will has
been the motivating factor in our part of the world. Empiri-
cism is the fruit of the fully developed will. Everything in the
West is substantiated by and finds its value in an *a priori* at-
mosphere. Every effect must have its measurable cause, otherwise it does not exist. Anything that cannot be measured by
this formula is fantasy, hallucination, misplaced logic, or just
plain stupidity. The suggestion of the ancients that there exists a ground of immediate knowledge, a dimension of experience superseding that of everyday consciousness has
been ignored by us since the advent of the experimental
method suggested by Descartes.

What has been spoiled by the father—the rational, determined approach of the experimental sciences—has been the
intuitive and suprarational intimations of a realm wherein
meaning exists beyond meaning. What has been spoiled by
the father is the ability to spontaneously accept the information inherent in that other realm of experience, the realm
from which the *I Ching* and other such devices speak.

When both the lower primary trigram and the lower nuclear trigram are viewed as changed, another nuclear hexagram to be considered emerges: Hexagram 53, Gradual Development:

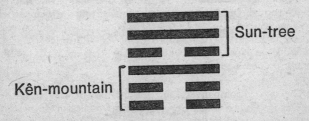

Sun-tree

Kên-mountain

Here again the tree is present, but this time it has risen to
the height of a mountain. The time of splitting apart is one
of contemplation and sacrifice, the successful completion of
which leads to a union of opposites, or the marriage of sun

and moon as shown in the heart of this hexagram:

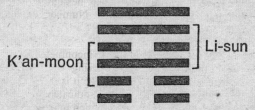

K'an-moon   Li-sun

The seeds of the future, the active light principle, must leave the field of action, or are in the act of leaving the field of action. They are about to enter the earth, about to have their light hidden or obscured. This time exists between the Hexagram of Splitting Apart, Number 23, and Return, Number 24. The hexagram that outlines the nature of such a time, a time when the light principle is hidden, is Hexagram 36, Darkening of the Light:

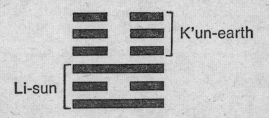

K'un-earth

Li-sun

The image is of the sun hidden beneath the earth. Interestingly enough the Sequence accompanying this hexagram tells us that whatever expands will of a certainty experience resistance and injury. This reminds us of the adornment, the attitude of expansiveness, which causes the time of splitting apart to come about.

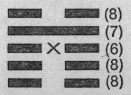

(8)
(7)
X (6)
(8)
(8)

The fifth line received was an 8:

Here we have the primary nuclear hexagram of the hexagram emerging. It is Obstruction, Number 39, of which Legge says:

> Ch'ien is the symbol of incompetency
> in the feet and legs, involving
> difficulty in walking; hence it is
> used in this hexagram to indicate
> a state of the kingdom which makes
> the government of it an arduous task.

(Difficulty in walking is also given us by the attributes of two trigrams: the upper primary trigram K'an [difficulty] and the upper nuclear trigram Li [a crab].)

The hexagrams of Splitting Apart and Obstruction are here intermingled. The judgment for Obstruction tells us that the southwest furthers, the northeast does not. The directions refer us to the diagram of later heaven or inner world arrangement.

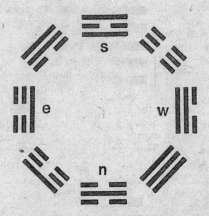

In the northeast stands the trigram Kên, which in this diagram, symbolizes the end of all things. The north, occupied by K'an, is the place of danger, winter, and midnight. The mountain is inaccessible and the path leading to it is dangerous. The judgment is trying to tell us that one must not continue climbing upward. The southwest is the place of K'un, the receptive and devoted principle. The north is the place of light and clarity occupied by the trigram Li, fire.

The image for Obstruction tells us that the man who is of a superior nature looks at himself and works on his character. When one can no longer move outward, when there is an obstruction, the only avenue left is the road leading in. The West, the United States of America is undergoing a tremendous transformation. The *Book of Changes* appears to be telling us that each individual must turn inward to make sure he is prepared for the new time. Through contemplating exterior events, the time of splitting apart, he learns that the time calls for change not only at the collective level, but at the personal level as well. The individual has two choices. He may continue on the path of the group, thereby making himself subject to the irrational impulses permeating society, attempting or learning to work creatively in the eye of the storm, or he may turn inward to work on himself.

If he chooses the latter course, he does not divorce himself from the world, from the field of activity, but aims to retain the individuality that is too often lost when working on the collective level. In the long run it is the individual and not the mass man who contributes to his culture. The individual's superiority expresses itself as the ability to be involved in the time without being swept away by it. The ground beneath his feet is neither a political platform that may at any moment be destroyed, carrying him along with it, nor an emotional and irrational attitude. His base is a human one because it is a total commitment to understanding not only the mechanics of exterior events, but the evolution of his own soul. This ability to be totally present to the inner as well as the outer world is what allows him to distinguish what is real and what is unreal. Because the *Book of Changes* addresses itself to the superior man, we must assume that it speaks to the potential hidden in each of us, and in addressing that potential attempts to bring it to fulfillment.

The *Book of Changes* tells us that the time of splitting apart has come for the West and that the only thing the individual can do now is contemplate not only the situation, but himself. To push upward and onward is to bring ruin. The time of splitting apart is a natural event in world history. It will pass and then society will have to be restructured. Only the man who has not wasted his energies will be capable of aiding in this great task. The individual need not lend himself to this work unless he knows he has really been called upon to do so. If he has not, he may be assured that the time will complete itself without any human intervention. It is important that things fall into decay because then the cycle of rebirth begins. It is also important that at the beginning there be men who have survived the cataclysm and who have a firm foothold on that which is indestructible, that which is truly theirs and cannot be taken from them—the firm ground of awareness and consciousness of those who have discovered that all revolutions have their origin in the soul of man, and that once the interior revolt has been brought to a standstill nothing that may approach them in the world can shake them.

The last nuclear hexagram is composed of the lower primary trigram, K'un, and the upper nuclear trigram, K'an. It is the hexagram of Holding Together, Number 8.

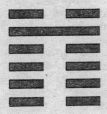

The Sequence for this hexagram tells us that in a great collective body there is certainly a reason for uniting, and that the time of holding together is the time of union. The hexagram is enmeshed with Splitting Apart, Obstruction, and Contemplation. At a time of splitting apart the individual, by contemplating the exterior event and his relation to it, recognizes the obstruction to individual advancement and retreats within himself to hold together. He who does this survives the exterior event. This is an easy thing for an Oriental to understand for he has methods of contemplation by which he may be guided. The Occidental has lost all vestiges of any such system of psychic reorganization. He is naked before the world and himself. Few guidelines are present. The *Book*

of Changes, however, by speaking of itself as a king who surveys the needs of his people, offers itself as a method of introspection whereby each individual may learn to discover his own interior guidelines. The important thing to do during the time of splitting apart and obstruction is to contemplate and hold together. The *I Ching* shows us how to survive the conflict of the opposites.

The last line received was an 8, leaving us with Hexagram 16, Enthusiasm, for our answer:

The Sequence for this hexagram tells us that when one possesses something great and knows how to be modest, one experiences enthusiasm. The great thing we possess is the *Book of Changes* itself. The third line, which is a moving line in our answer, reads: "When one is enthusiastic and looks upward, one creates remorse. Hesitation brings remorse." The subject of the line looks up and out to a leader. What need does he have of a leader? The book has already advised that the movement should be inward, not outward. To seek comfort in a leader is to lose one's individuality. Again, the book tells us that we must seek the superior man in ourselves.

This hexagram changes to Hexagram 62, Preponderance of the Small:

The miscellaneous notes appended to this hexagram inform us that the time of the hexagram signifies the time of transition, which we have already discussed in our analysis of the nuclear hexagram of Splitting Apart. But the judgment reveals that we have been on the right track: It tells us of a bird that brings the message that one should not strive upward at this time, but should remain below. What should predominate is the small, the seemingly insignificant. It is a time when one should not attempt to do great things. The time of this hexagram symbolizes a bird who flies too high. The message is that one should be in contact with the ground of one's own individual experience. In a difficult time of transition, the *I Ching* offers itself as a guide.

The proven method for self-mastery and success in career and personal life . . .

THE POWER OF WORDS IN YOUR LIFE

Elizabeth R. Hogan

"The difference between the right word and almost the right word is the difference between lightning and the lightning bug."

—Mark Twain

Language—the tool of communication—can be the most important influence in your life. *What* you say and *how* you say it clearly mirror your state of mind, disposition and education.

Language permits one person to place his ideas at the disposal of another. Verbal and written communication precedes, accompanies and follows almost all human activity. The correct use of words can enlarge and enrich life—let it enlarge and enrich yours.

A553—75¢

A panoramic guide to forbidden erotic works...

THE ENCYCLOPEDIA OF EROTICA

Edited by Dr. Paul J. Gillette

Artworks whose primary focus is on sexual desire, activity or behavior, selected by the editor as significant examples of erotic literature, comprise the selection of erotica in this collection.

Ranging from classics to best-selling novels of today, this fantastic volume contains, in their entirety, long-suppressed works like Ovid's *Art of Love*, Mark Twain's *1601*, de Maupassant's *Forbidden Fruit*, as well as lengthy excerpts from well-known books (*The Memoirs of Dolly Morton, Grushenka, City of Night, Candy*) and underground classics (*White Thighs, The Whipping Club, The Virgin of Orleans, The Amours of a Musical Student*). A497–$1.50